helper *by design*

Elyse Fitzpatrick

helper *by design*

God's Perfect Plan for Women in Marriage

Elyse Fitzpatrick

MOODY PUBLISHERS
CHICAGO

Cover Design: Ragont Design
Cover photography: © Eric Schmidt/Masterfile

ISBN: 0-8024-0869-9

1 3 5 7 9 10 8 6 4 2
Printed in the United States of America

To Anita Manata and Donna Turner,
sweet sisters, companions, counselors, and helpers.
Your prayers and love of the truth are among the most
precious gifts I've been given.
What a joy will be ours as we worship our King together!

Contents

Acknowledgments

Words are insufficient to express the gratitude that I have for those who have helped me in this project. I am blessed to know so many godly people and to have the privilege to ask them hard questions and to rest, knowing that they're praying for me.

Among those who particularly helped me in the process of writing this book are:

- Craig Cabaniss, my pastor at Grace Church (Sovereign Grace Ministries), who read every chapter and offered humble and gentle criticisms;

- Dennis E. Johnson and Iain Duguid, my professors-on-tap at Westminster Theological Seminary (Escondido, California); and Iain's wife (and my pal), Barbara, for saving me from theological error and always being available to me so that I could ask my goofy questions;

- Wayne and Kei Laliberte and the group that meets in their house (Phil, Lawrence and Eda, Brad and Dawn, Scott and Joci, Bev, and Cody and Jessica), for their encouragement, lively discussion, and especially for their faithful prayer;

- the dear women who join me on Thursday nights for book club (especially Lori Ann, Donna, Sandy, Rachel, Leanna, Chelsea, Julie, Bev, Kathie, Annie, and Jessica), for their theological acumen and godly lives that strengthen and encourage me;

- John Hickernell and the staff at Evangelical Bible Book Store (as always);

- Carol Cornish and Martha Peace, my cross-country counselors and friends;

- Wayne Grudem, John Piper, Werner Neuer, Susan Hunt, Beth Impson, Elizabeth George, Anthony Hoekema, Alexander Strauch, John Benton and John MacAruthur Jr., whose books I devoured in my background reading;

- Elsa Mazon and Moody Publishers for believing that women want to read theologically strong books about God's call on their life.

Thanks go as well to two other persons whose work is especially reflected in two of the chapters: Tambra Murphy, whose insights into ungodly truces in marriage appear in chapter 12; and Pastor Dave Eby of North City Presbyterian Church, in Poway, California, for his insightful sermons on the topic of submission, which I used extensively in chapter 9, "Learning the Steps of the Dance."

Finally, heartfelt thanks must go to my family, particularly my husband, Phil, who helped me in ways too numerous to mention (not the least of which is continuing to love me year after year); to my dear mother, Rosemary, who edited every chapter; to James, Cody, and Jessica; Joel and Ruth (and Ruth's father, George Scipione); and to Wesley and Hayden (my darlings) for loving me and teaching me what it means to be a woman created in the image of God.

Preface

This is my seventh book, although I have to admit that it would be more fitting if it were my tenth. That's because the number seven is thought by some to represent perfection whereas the number ten symbolizes trials. I say that this should be my tenth book because it has been the most difficult book I've written. Honestly, there were days I strongly considered forsaking the whole project. Then, when by God's mercy, I once again regained forward motion, I felt I was walking in the dark . . . trying to learn what I just tripped over, picking up a stone, holding it . . . examining it, experiencing it. What does the heat of this rock mean? Is it really blistering hot or is it just that my hands are so cold? Is it genuinely sharp? Does it have to cut, or am I just hanging on to it too tightly or holding it in the wrong places? Couldn't I just describe it for you, as an impersonal bystander, and avoid placing it in my own heart?

In some ways my previous six books were about my own personal struggles and my search for victory in them—some struggles being more personal and painful than others. This book is just like that for me . . . only more so.

As I set out to write on this topic, I originally saw it as an interesting jaunt down a theological bypath. Then I discovered that I was going to have to suffer the walk down that path, and this writing became intensely personal and painful for me. The Lord has obliged me to shine light on areas in my own life that I've historically neglected. I discovered that I needed to work through these issues for myself, for my marriage. There was much that desperately needed to be redeemed. For me, the darkness on my path wasn't only a matter of ignorance or misinformation. It was also a matter of unbelief and sinful rebellion on my part. So, although this manuscript isn't primarily a description of my journey toward wholeness and holiness, it is that.

In trying to write personally and share my heart with you, I've had to traverse another thorny path: I've wanted to let you see me and learn how I've fought to flesh out Truth, but I haven't wanted to be so candid that my dear husband was denigrated in any way. I respect and love Phil and admire him especially for the patience he's had in sacrificially shepherding me for all these years. If you knew him, you would respect and love him, too.

Even though I've reached one objective because now you hold this book in your hands, I want you to know that I haven't arrived at our true destination yet. I'm not Mrs. Proverbs 31 or the Total Woman, but I do have a clearer picture of where I'm headed and how to get there. I trust this book will paint that picture for you.

Thank you, dear sisters, for joining me in this journey. I respect your love for God's glory and your desire to grow in His calling more than you'll ever know.

Elyse Fitzpatrick
Escondido, California
2003

Introduction

SOMETHING MORE THAN TEA AND COOKIES?

Teresa sat in my office, as she had for a number of weeks, listening to counsel, asking questions. The trouble she faced in her daily life was a result of her own mistakes, the abuse she suffered as a child, her former lesbian relationships, and problems with her husband. She was confused and despairing, and seemed to me to be a mere shadow of a woman: her dress, her demeanor shouted, "I'm not one of you!"

On this occasion, she spoke of her inability to relate to the other women in her congregation. She felt like an outcast. She experienced an incessant alienation from other women. She found herself fearful, jealous, angry, and bitter, and yet she admitted that she also longed to be part of the group. She was confused about her role in the home; she wondered how embracing her role as helper might transform her.

"I don't do cookies," she stated. Her tone was one of defiance, but her face spoke of fear and sadness. "Do I have to?"

WHERE ARE YOU STARTING?

Perhaps as you read Teresa's story, you see yourself and recognize that you've had the same kinds of questions. Teresa's confusion isn't really about cookies, is it? What she's really asking is, "What does it mean to be a Christian woman?"

On the other hand, you might have read about Teresa with curiosity, not relating to her thoughts and feelings at all. Perhaps you see yourself more as the kind of woman who really does love to bake cookies and have tea parties, but still you have questions: "Is there something more to being my husband's helper than preparing his meals and cleaning his house?" Perhaps you've even wondered whether God's design for women intersects with your natural inclination as a homemaker.

In the chapters to come, together we'll discover what it means to be a companion and helper. We'll learn how to pursue oneness with our spouses without losing sight of our individuality, and we'll take a watchful stroll down the often-perilous path of biblical submission. In all these endeavors you'll find encouragement to become aware of what it means to be a woman created in the image of God, a woman who has been designed to be a helper and a companion, and you'll learn the sweet pleasures embodied in that calling.

I recognize that even among Christian women there is a great divergence of opinion on this topic and that these opinions range across a broad spectrum. Some women sincerely believe that a June Cleaver or a Martha Stewart is the quintessential model of God's created role for a woman. Still others think that there are no intrinsic differences between men and women except that a woman is housed in a body that menstruates, lactates, and gestates—something that no man (aside from Arnold Swartzenegger) ever did.

ELUCIDATING THE FEMININE ESSENCE

From ages past, men and women have been trying to define what it means to be a godly woman. Lemuel, the mysterious writer of Proverbs 31, defined her in terms of faithfulness, industry, strength, kindness, and inner beauty. Where did he learn his definition of the "virtuous woman"? From his mother, of course (Proverbs 31:1).

In some ways it might be easy simply to define women on the basis of their life roles: *wife, daughter, sister, mother, aunt, grandmother.* But is there something beyond these roles? Is there a basic something that defines a *woman* as a woman that would make her different from a man even if she weren't married and didn't have children or siblings? As author Carol Cornish says of these terms, "Those words describe a role, not an identity. If you are suddenly injured or otherwise incapable of fulfilling your main role in life, then, do you lose your identity? Suppose you go into a coma. Who are you then?"[1]

A HELPMEET? *A WHAT?*

From the very earliest days of my Christian life, I've heard that I'm supposed to be a helpmeet (a reference to Genesis 2:18 in the KJV). I'll be honest with you. I've been married for nearly thirty years now, have been a Christian even longer, and until the last few years, I never did any intentional thinking about what the term *helpmeet* really meant. It was just one of those Christian terms that was very familiar but empty of solid content. I could have told you I was supposed to be one, but aside from some very general categories, I couldn't have told you with any precision what that meant: Bearing children? Washing the bathroom floor? Having dinner ready promptly at six o'clock?

In addition, I admit I can't remember giving any serious thought to what it meant to reflect God's image as a woman; how could I, a *her*, reflect *His* image? I did recognize that God's work to change me meant that I would become more like Jesus Christ, but aside from that, I have to admit that I've been pretty much in the dark.

WHERE I'M COMING FROM

Before we begin to explore together what it means to be a help-meet, I want to help you understand where I'm coming from, because as we share our time together, you'll see that I have certain biases that color my thinking and guide my conclusions. Think of these beliefs as the undergirding of all that I'll propose here.

- *The Bible is our guide.* God, (the Father, Son, and Holy Spirit) has revealed Himself to mankind most clearly through the Bible. So if we want to know about who God is, what He's doing, and what pleases Him, we'll need to look to His Word. After all, it will be impossible to reflect Him if our picture of Him is false.

  In addition, because God is our all-knowing and all-wise Creator, it also makes sense that we look to the Bible when we think about who we are as women. As we look deeply into Scripture, we'll begin to understand the truth about ourselves, who we are, why we're here, what He's called us to, and how to change. There is much in evangelical tradition about the roles of women, and I hope to affirm what is truly biblical while avoiding what is not. In this book, we'll start (and stay) with biblical descriptions and categories.

- *Our primary call is to reflect His Son.* Jesus Christ, God's only Son, came to earth as a man, lived a perfectly sinless life, suffered God's wrath by being executed as a criminal in our place, rose from the dead, and ascended to heaven. Not only is trust in His sacrifice essential for eternal life, it's also the only way to be freed from sin and enabled to grow in mirroring Him. (If you're not sure that you're a Christian, please turn to appendix A). I'm resting in the knowledge that it's not my place to try to coerce or convince you to make changes in your life.

Our change rests solely in His love for us, His bride, and His desire to make us beautiful. He's committed Himself to that process, all for His glory and our great joy.

- *We need God's grace and power.* God's Word is a rich storehouse of wisdom, but that wisdom means nothing if we're not willing to submit ourselves to it. Only those who, by His grace, willingly bow at His throne and submit their lives to Him are able to benefit from what God says in His Word. What's more, we'll never attain this humble heart-attitude without the help of the Holy Spirit. He calls us to reflect Him, and then He works in our hearts to desire to do so and enables us to grow. This life-changing wisdom is available to everyone who has bowed before the Lord, no matter that person's gender, age, race, basic intelligence, family heritage, or social status. The Holy Spirit is an equal-opportunity illuminator: working powerfully in the hearts of all those who have responded in faith to God's gracious call.

OUR CALLING

The Bible was written, in part, to inform us of God's plan for our lives. It tells us who we are, what our goals should be, what God's plan is, and what He's created us to do. I'll refer to this body of information as a woman's calling. I know that people usually use the term *calling* more narrowly, to refer to being called into the ministry or some employment. A pastor might say, "I first felt God's calling to enter the ministry when I was sixteen." In the following pages I'll use this term more broadly. I'll use it to mean everything I am as a woman, including my soul, my desires, my aspirations, my inclinations, my physiology, my employments: in essence, who God created me to be, or *my identity.*

WHO ARE WE?

When we look to the Bible to learn about our calling, we don't have to read very far before we hit pay dirt. In the first few chapters of Genesis, we can find almost everything we need to know to begin to steer our thinking in the right direction. So, as we embark on our study, we're going to look at several passages from Genesis about God's image in us and particularly our calling as women. Then, once we've built that foundation, we'll look more specifically at our calling as companions and helpers in the areas of oneness, submission, communication, and hope-filled obedience.

Where do you find yourself today? Are you like Teresa—angry, bitter, alienated, and confused? Or do you see yourself as more compliant while at the same time seeking a broader comprehension of your call? Perhaps you've picked up this book without much hope of having a better marriage, having settled into a benign resignation. The delightful truth is that wherever you find yourself today, God, the great Heart-Changer, has committed Himself to your good and to completing the work He has begun in His people (Philippians 1:6 NKJV), all for His ultimate glory. So let me invite you to join me, wherever you are in this process, as we grow together into the women He's called us to be.

chapter 1 In His Image

*"God created man in His own image . . . male
and female He created them."*

∽ GENESIS 1:27

In the past three years, I've been blessed in many ways, one of those ways being the gift of our two little grandsons, Wesley and Hayden. During this time, my husband and I have had the opportunity to rediscover the joy of having little ones around. We had no idea how splendid being grandparents would be . . . little toothless smiles, halting steps, ticklish toes, bright eyes.

Our little Hayden (who isn't yet a year old at this writing) has bonded with my husband, Phil (a.k.a. "Poppie"). Hayden loves him, and whenever Poppie is around, he just naturally gravitates toward him. Phil's in love, too. "Want me to hold the boy?" he asks. That's Phil-speak for "Please give me the baby right now, before I grab him."

Poppie and Hayden frequently take little strolls through our backyard. They look at leaves. They touch the flowers. They watch the birdies in the bird feeders. They are discovering the world: Hayden for the first time, Poppie anew.

WHAT DO YOU SEE?

When you look at the world, what do you see? When the sky blazes in dazzling golden scarlet, when you hear the silence of a snowfall, or dive under a wave as it crashes powerfully over your body, what are you aware of?

When you watch a little toddler try to stack colored rings in the right order or when an ice skater finally lands that quadruple jump and the crowd erupts in cheers, do you know what you are seeing?

Do you see God's hand everywhere? Do you see His fingerprint on this world? Lofty mountains, verdant trees, azure sky, fertile earth . . . the smell of gardenias, the gurgle of a baby's laugh all speak loudly to those who are listening. Do you hear? Do you really see?

Earth's crammed with heaven
And every common bush afire with God:
But only he who sees, takes off his shoes,
The rest sit round it, and pluck blackberries,
And daub their natural faces unaware.[1]

Earth is crammed with heaven. Think on those words. In everything you see, do you really see? Are you aware of the Author's presence? Do you "take off your shoes" because you know you're standing on holy ground? Or are you busy gobbling up those yummy blackberries and then trying to tidy up afterwards?

Growing in the understanding of God's pervasive direction on our calling begins with a journey back to the book of beginnings, back to Genesis.

MEN AND WOMEN IN GOD'S IMAGE

"Then God said, 'Let Us make man in Our image, according to

Our likeness.' . . . God created man in His own image, in the image of God He created him; male and female He created them" (Genesis 1:26–27).

What does it mean to be created in God's "image"? The Hebrew word that's translated "image" in this verse (*tselem*) is the same word that's used to describe idols, images that are made to *represent* false gods. (It is interesting, isn't it, that God creates man in His image and man then seeks to create false images of God?) Another word that's used in the verses above, "likeness" (*demūth*), is a word that simply means "to be like." All humanity (men and women), then, are *equally* representations of God and are like Him in certain aspects. (In subsequent chapters, we'll look at how the image of God in man was shattered in the Fall and how the image is being restored to believers in Christ.) But just what does that mean? In what ways are we like God? After all, there are some very definite differences between Him and us. How are we similar? Perhaps an illustration will help.

As I sit here writing in my cozy little office, I've got pictures of my family all around. I've got a picture of one son with his new, lovely bride. I've got a sweet picture of our daughter, when she was playing varsity softball, standing with Phil, who was an assistant coach. I've got another picture of our whole family—with both of our dear sons and our son-in-law—which we took at my in-law's fiftieth wedding anniversary. I can sit and stare at these pictures and they bring back wonderful memories of sweet joys. But as much as I love these pictures, I have to say that they are just images. They are representations of what the family looked like a few years ago. They are not the real thing, although they are real representations.

In some ways, men and women are images of God the way that these pictures are images of our family. The pictures look similar, but they lack the depth, the animation, the life of the real people. You would wonder about my mental health if I sat around talking to my pictures or kissing them (like I did my autographed picture of the Beatles when I was a teenager) because they aren't the "real thing."

Although there are differences between our kids and their pictures, there are also similarities. You can get a little bit of an understanding of what the family looks like, and maybe even a little glimpse of how we interact, when you look at our pictures. And of course, the pictures themselves do capture certain visual aspects of their subjects.

What's more, we're always very pleased when we get our pictures back and they look just like reality as we remember it. "This looks just like you," we happily say. We love pictures that accurately freeze one moment of time and help us see what is no longer visible.

GOD'S PORTRAIT PAINTED THROUGHOUT THE UNIVERSE

The Bible teaches that God possesses some qualities that belong to Him alone and other qualities that He shares. Some of the attributes God alone possesses include His infinity, changelessness, immensity, sovereignty, and freedom. God is also a Spirit, which means that He isn't limited by time or space. The attributes or qualities He shares in some measure with humanity include His holiness, righteousness, truth, love, mercy, patience, and goodness.

Thus people reflect or picture some of God's characteristics. I say that we reflect *some* of His attributes because even before sin entered the world, there was a great difference between our Creator and us, much like the difference between my family and their portraits. Before we look at the similarities between the Lord and ourselves, let's examine two of the differences.

HE'S THE CREATOR

God is the Creator, and we are His creation. He's absolutely independent, needing nothing to sustain His life. We're dependent upon Him for our very life. This vast difference will never change—even when we're in heaven and we enjoy unhindered fellowship with Him. There will always be a distinction between us. Paul preached about this when he stood at the base of the Parthenon, where the Greeks worshiped their idols, on Mars Hill:

The God who made the world and all things in it, since He is Lord of heaven and earth, does not dwell in temples made with hands; nor is He served by human hands, as though He needed anything, since He Himself gives to all people life and breath and all things. (Acts 17:24–25)

We need both the material creation (air, water, food, clothing) and people (in the sense that we need to love others and to learn from them) in order to survive. We're dependent upon God for everything.

HE'S SOVEREIGN

God is also the only One who always does exactly what He wants to do. The psalmist wrote, "Our God is in the heavens; He does whatever He pleases" (Psalm 115:3). God is completely sovereign, which means that He rules as the King of all His creation, doing exactly what He wants when He wants. I know that even though I'm created in His image, I can't do whatever I want whenever I want (although I frequently forget this fact when zooming down the freeway).

Next we'll look at some of the qualities we have in common with God.

HE'S HOLY

God is holy in all He is and does. The Bible says that His holiness is so great it's "majestic" (Exodus 15:11)! And every day, He's exactly the same (because there is no "day" with Him). That God is holy means two things: First, that God is "other." He's different, He's weighty, He's not a vapor, He doesn't change. In this aspect of holiness, we're not like Him at all. But holiness has another meaning:

moral purity. We can't share in the first sense of His holiness—His "otherness"—but we can share in His virtue.

HE'S PERFECT IN EVERY WAY

God sees things as they really are; in fact, He understands everything about everything. Not only is our perception flawed, but even when we do observe correctly, our understanding of what we're seeing isn't always right. But God is different, as the psalmist writes: "Great is our Lord . . . His understanding is infinite" (Psalm 147:5). Knowledge, wisdom, and understanding are traits that God has shared with us.

God is also perfect in righteousness. That means that His character matches His perfect standard. Toward the end of his life, Moses sang of God's righteousness, "The Rock! His work is perfect, for all His ways are just; . . . righteous and upright is He" (Deuteronomy 32:4). God's righteousness was perfectly displayed for us in the life of Jesus Christ. It's this righteousness that's been credited to us as Christians, as Paul wrote: "He made Him who knew no sin to be sin on our behalf, so that we might become the righteousness of God in Him" (2 Corinthians 5:21). So, again, in one sense we share in God's righteousness, but in another sense we're growing in it. We can rejoice today that the Lord never fails in His work to transform and enlighten His children.

Finally, God is perfect in His love. In fact, John teaches that if you want to know what love really looks like, you have to look at God because "God *is* love" (1 John 4:8, italics added). Human love has boundaries, but God's love is so far-reaching that He sacrificed His one and only Son, the Son He loved, to bless those who hated Him. That kind of love amazes me! Our love for Him and for others will grow as we meditate on and seek to reflect His love for us to others. But He hasn't abandoned us or left us to accomplish this great love on our own. The Bible says that the "love of God has been poured out within our hearts through the Holy Spirit" (Romans 5:5).

GOD'S IMAGE EVERYWHERE

Aside from these moral qualities, are there other areas in which *everyone* reflects God's image? John Calvin writes that the image of God with which Adam

> was endowed is expressed by this word, when he had full possession of right understanding, when he had his affections kept within the bounds of reason, all his senses tempered in right order, and he truly referred his excellence to exceptional gifts bestowed upon him by his Maker. And although the primary seat of the divine image was in the mind and heart, or in the soul and its powers, *yet there was no part of man, not even the body itself, in which some sparks did not glow.*[2]

Let's look at what God called Adam and Eve to do when He first created them in order to get a sense of how they were to represent or image Him.

RULING LIKE HIM

God's first call to Adam and Eve was for them to rule over the creation. In ruling, they were being like God. God rules sovereignly over all creation as a great King, as 1 Chronicles 29:11 says: "Yours, O Lord, is the greatness and the power and the glory and the victory and the majesty, indeed everything that is in the heavens and the earth; Yours is the dominion, O Lord, and You exalt Yourself as head over all."

Although we don't rule sovereignly, both Adam *and* Eve were called to rule under God's jurisdiction. In the Psalms, David wonders at the great privilege that's ours in representing God in this way. "What is man that You take thought of him? . . .You make him to rule over the works of Your hands; You have put all things under his feet" (Psalm 8:4, 6).

After God created Adam, He planted a special place for him to dwell: a beautiful mountaintop garden. He then placed Adam there and gave him a specific calling. He was to cultivate and keep the garden. Adam also ruled over creation by naming all the animals and by observing the seasons and the world that God had created. God called him to subdue all of creation for his own use and God's glory.

We continue to rule over creation even today. Men and women explore the nature of hurricanes, examine microbes, repave streets, work to make life better. Why? Because of God's imprint on our souls. We're fulfilling God's calling. Just think about it: even little children reflect God when they build sand castles or explore the shore for seashells. When we're involved in honorable work, even if it doesn't directly consist of Christian ministry, we're mirroring one of God's attributes. Why? Because God works and rules. Men and women are called to be God's coregents, working and ruling in His world, under His authority, for our happiness and His glory. Wives who are helping their husbands rule are also growing in God's call. Not only do we reflect Him when we rule over the world, we also associate with others as He does.

RELATING LIKE HIM

God created Adam and Eve as male and female. He could have made two men or even another sort of creature for Adam, but instead He created one who was like Adam in his humanness, yet differing from him both in his physique and calling.

As we ponder this truth, it becomes apparent that God loves variety. In fact, variety itself reflects God's image. Remember who He is? He says that He is a Trinity: One God, three persons. There aren't three Fathers, or three Sons. No, God in His perfection is diverse, yet the same. God the Father, Son, and Holy Spirit are all the same in their being (all equally God), yet different in their functions.

These differences are seen in creation itself. God the *Father* spoke the world into existence, but it was God the *Son* who was the Word carrying out His decrees. God the *Spirit* moved over the waters, "sustaining and manifesting God's immediate presence in His creation."[3] We see this diversity in our redemption, as well. For God the "Father planned redemption and sent His Son into the world [and] the Holy Spirit was sent by the Father and the Son to apply redemption to us."[4] Do you see how the members of the Trinity are the same (equally and fully God) and yet different (with differing functions or roles)?

Men and women are similar to God in that aspect. We are the same (equally and fully human and in His image) and yet we are different (with both similar and differing callings). (We're going to look very deeply at the differences in our callings in chapter 2.) Isn't God's wisdom amazing? This point will be very important when we talk about a woman's specific calling as a helper in the next chapter. For now, though, just remember that both *men and women are the same in essence* (as are the members of the Godhead) and that we have differing callings (also as God does), although both men and women are called first to glorify and enjoy God and reflect Him to the rest of His creation.

REPRODUCING LIKE HIM

Third, God called Adam and Eve to be "fruitful and multiply, and fill the earth" (Genesis 1:28). In doing that, they were being like Him because that's just what He did. From His person a world sprang forth in His likeness, filled with His children. Paul called people the "children of God" when he was preaching to the unbelieving Greeks about creation: "The God who made the world and all things in it . . . .gives to all people life and breath and all things; and He made from one man every nation of mankind to live on all the face of the earth . . . being then the children of God" (Acts 17:24–26, 29).

There is a difference, of course, between those who are generally part of humanity and those who are specifically part of God's redeemed family. All humans are His children in the sense that they are created in His image and that He lovingly sustains their lives. Only believers, however, can claim to be God's children in the sense that they are in relation with Him as their Father.

God has invited us to reflect Him by having children. Similar to Him, we have children after our likeness. People reproduce in other ways aside from having children, too. We teach, mentor, and disciple others who are not directly a part of our biological family.

Of course, here's another place where our differences are very plain. God creates; we do not. We procreate after our likeness, but we don't come up with something that's completely new, nor do we create something out of nothing simply by the word of our power. But still, the picture is there, isn't it?

REFLECTING LIKE HIM

On the sixth day of creation, God reflected on what He had done and pronounced it "very good" (Genesis 1:31). Like Him, we reflect on or ponder the rightness of all we see. In fact, that's something we do all the time. The outrage we experience while viewing pictures of the Holocaust mirrors God's moral judgments. Not only do we reflect in this way, we almost always communicate these thoughts (just as God did when He said that His creation was "very good"). Of course, God's judgment is never wrong, and ours may be, but the ability to discern and reflect is like Him.

Isn't it amazing that after He pronounced everything "good" at creation, God declared that there was something in His world that was "not good"? What was the one detail that lacked His approval? God declared that it wasn't good for Adam to be alone: "Then the Lord God said, 'It is *not good* for the man to be alone; I will make him a helper suitable for him'" (Genesis 2:18; italics added). So He took steps to remedy the situation—He created Eve, similar to the way that we want to correct situations that we deem unhappy or lacking.

By the way, God wasn't taken by surprise at Adam's need for a helper. He didn't think, *Oops! I better make a woman!* God waited until Adam discerned what he needed, after he had observed all the animals (Genesis 2:20). God had always planned to make men *and* women because men and women *together* reflect His nature of diversity and unity. We can be sure that God planned to make both men and women before He created Adam because we (redeemed men and women) were chosen in Him *"before* the foundation of the world" (Ephesians 1:4, italics added). (We'll look more deeply into Eve's creation in chapter 2.)

REJOICING LIKE HIM

After all of the time that Adam must have spent observing the animals, seeing them in pairs, and reflecting on his own lack of one that corresponded to him, it shouldn't be surprising that the very first statement we hear from Adam is one of praise and rejoicing. Adam said, "This *at last* is bone of my bones and flesh of my flesh; she shall be called Woman because she was taken out of Man" (Genesis 2:23, italics added).[5]

The ability and desire to praise what brings us pleasure is simply a reflection of the adoration that has always existed within the Trinity. As John Piper writes, God "rejoiced in the image of His glory in the person of His Son."[6] God revels in goodness (Hebrews 2:12), and because He does, so do we.

RESTING LIKE HIM

The creation story ends with God observing all that He had done and pronouncing it "very good" (Genesis 1:31). God completed all His work in six days, and on the seventh He rested as He observed the wisdom and magnificence of all that He had done. He then set the seventh day apart by blessing it as a time for the most special and pleasing enjoyment of man: to revel in the sweet joy of fellowship with his Creator and to observe His great acts. When Adam and Eve were commanded to observe the Sabbath rest they weren't told to spend the day napping. They were to spend it in communion with their Lord and enjoyment of one another.

HIS ABIDING IMAGE

Are you beginning to see how God's image permeates all His creation? His image permeates men and women in ways we've only just begun to see in this chapter. He's called us to rule, relate, reproduce, reflect, rejoice, and rest like Him. Not only does His image fill all the world and everyone in it, but it is particularly being re-created in those of us who are His redeemed children. This should cause your heart to be filled with confidence. If God could imprint His image on all mankind one day thousands of years ago, so that we perpetually reflect Him even now, then He can flood your heart and change you to be more and more like Him today.

We've just begun to see how we already reflect God's image, and I trust that these pictures have created a fresh vision and hope for growth in your heart. God remains faithful, and He'll give us everything we need to grow into our calling as women and helpers. Take a few moments now, though, to reflect on the ways that the world reflects Him and allow your heart to rejoice in your great King.

Finding and Fulfilling Your Calling

1. Review the five Rs that point out how all God's children image Him. In what ways do you see yourself, as a woman, doing this? In what ways is thinking in this way new for you?

a. Ruling over creation. *Frequently your specific gifting is key to your call to rule. We can't rule over everything in the world, nor are we called to. We are called, however, to be faithful to rule within the sphere of influence and with the specific giftings He's given us. How can you use your gifting to bring your garden under God's dominion?*

b. Relating to other people. *Ask yourself: "How am I furthering God's reign in my relationships with others, particularly my husband? How can I help him relate to others in a more God-honoring way?"*

c. Reproducing others. *Ask yourself, "Whom has God placed in my life for me to nurture?" This should be more than natural children, although the nurturing of children is a major facet of this calling. What qualities of the Spirit is God working in you? How can you reproduce that in others?*

d. Reflecting on God and the creation around you. *Ask yourself: "How am I growing in loving God with all my mind? What areas of interest has God given me that I might pursue for His glory and the good of others?"*

e. Rejoicing in Him. *Ask yourself: "What divine qualities are most precious to me? How much time do I spend meditating on God's character and then praising Him for who He is? Is my life marked by joy or drudgery?"*

f. Resting in communion with Him. *If you feel that you don't have time to do any of the above, may I suggest that you begin to look at the Sabbath as the great day when you can return (in a sense) to the garden to walk with Him and enjoy His presence and rule in your life?*

2. *Begin to think about what it means to you, as a woman, to rule, in light of the fact that you're also called to be a helper. Write out your thoughts.*

3. *How does the unity and diversity of the Trinity impact your view of yourself as a woman? Do you really rejoice in God's love of variety?*

4. *First Corinthians 13:12 says, "For now we see in a mirror dimly, but then face to face; now I know in part, but then I will know fully just as I also have been fully known." We dimly reflect or grasp the wonder of God's majesty and glory here on earth. The Bible teaches, though, that there will come a day when we will see Him face-to-face and know Him more fully. Write out a prayer of rejoicing as you anticipate that day.*

5. *I frequently find myself reading through a chapter of a book without being aware of what's written there. So I've found that it's helpful to try to summarize the teaching of the chapter in three or four points before I leave it and forget what I just read. May I encourage you to do the same at the end of every chapter? That way you'll compel yourself to think more deeply about the main themes of the book, and you'll have a record of what you're learning.*

chapter 2   # His Companion, His Helper

And the Lord God said, "It isn't good for man
to be alone; I will make a companion for him,
a helper suited to his needs."

∽ GENESIS 2:18 TLB

J ennie had come to me for a number of weeks for help in her
marriage when I asked her to contemplate how God meant
for her to be a companion and helper to her husband. I requested
that she think specifically about the ramifications of God giving her
to her husband so that he would not be alone.

"Well," she said, "our schedules are really very similar, so we do
spend a lot of time together. I don't see how he could say that he was
alone."

As we continued our discussion, it became apparent to both Jennie
and me that even though she was there physically with her husband,
the purposeful intimacy that conquers loneliness really wasn't occur-
ring. In addition, she had never thought about her calling to help her
husband by partnering with him in his endeavors to fulfill God's call
on his life. Being a companion-helper to her husband was something
that she had never really spent much time thinking deeply about.

Perhaps you can relate to Jennie's mystification. It may be that like her, you've never done any serious thinking about what your calling as a companion and helper ought to look like. It's very easy for us to just go about our lives, day by day, without ever stopping to consider just what it is that we're doing besides trying to get the laundry done before the soccer game and checking the date on the milk carton and wondering why it's already gone sour. The mundane operations of a household are certainly necessary and really are meaningful, but unless they're bolstered by concrete knowledge of biblical truth and your calling, these chores can seem pointless and superficial. Is there meaning behind it all? Is there a calling that will fulfill the deepest longings of our hearts? Just why did God give Adam a wife?

LIFE ALONE IS NOT GOOD

In this chapter we'll consider our creation and calling as wives more closely. Let me remind you again of God's pronouncement when He created the first wife, Eve. He said, "It is not good for the man to be alone; I will make him a helper suitable for him" (Genesis 2:18).

Have you ever thought about God's purpose in creating Eve for Adam? Let me remind you of the circumstances that surrounded her creation. In the midst of the unimaginable beauty of the garden, the lush trees and sparkling waters, an environment literally overflowing with God's matchless creative power, something existed that was "not good."

In the Hebrew there are two ways of saying that something is "not good." You can say that something is lacking in good ('ēn tôb): "like a meal without salt, or coffee without sugar. [In this usage], something is missing, without which the thing is not as good as it could be."[1] Or you can say that something is positively bad (lō'tôb), which is the case with the Hebrew used here. Man's situation without companionship, his aloneness, isn't simply lacking something

34

that might have made it better. No, without companionship,

> life can have no goodness. . . . Man was not created for solitude. . . .
> Man was not meant to be alone in the beginning, and he will not be
> alone in the end. Think of the description of heaven . . . Jesus has gone
> to prepare for us places at a feast, that most communal of activities.[2]

So "the Lord God fashioned into a woman the rib which He had taken from the man, and brought her to the man" (Genesis 2:22). Eve complemented Adam physically, intellectually, and morally because she was made from him. She wasn't exactly like him; rather, she corresponded to him in the same way that two pieces of a jigsaw puzzle fit together.

Adam stood out from the rest of the animal kingdom because God had breathed into him the "breath of life," something He did not do for any other animal. Remember, regarding no other part of creation do we hear the words, "made . . . in the likeness of God" (Genesis 5:1). Adam and Eve were unique in the creation, and although he was made from the dust of the earth (and Eve wasn't), she complemented and corresponded to him. Eve wasn't some other sort of creature; she wasn't beneath Adam, nor was she superior to him; but rather she was created as his partner, equally in God's image and called to glorify Him.

GOD'S FELLOWSHIP WITH HIMSELF

Just what was it about Adam's aloneness that was not good? The answer to this question is discovered in remembering that Adam was made to reflect God to the rest of the creation. So the lack in his solitude existed first in the fact that a solitary being (one alone) cannot adequately reflect our triune God (three in one). The mutual love, honor, purposeful accomplishment, and communal joy (in the midst of diversity) that we see in the Godhead could not begin to be experienced or displayed by one man alone. It would be impossible for Adam to rightly reflect God as a solitary being, for God is in union with Himself, and thus Adam needed to be in union with another.

ADAM'S FELLOWSHIP WITH ANOTHER

Although Adam knew unhindered fellowship with the Lord, walking with Him in the cool of the day, this vertical communion wasn't enough for God's purposes (apart from special giftings as Matthew 19:12 and 1 Corinthians 7:32–35 explain). As Jay Adams says, "Adam was not fashioned for solitary, isolated living. From the beginning his capacity for language, his walks and talks with God . . . and God's expressed concern that he not remain alone are all explicit evidences of the social side of human nature."[3]

Further, Adam's aloneness was not good because there weren't any other creatures with whom he could share his calling to rule, relate, reproduce, reflect, rejoice, and rest. He was incomplete without someone who could understand what this calling meant and who would encourage him and work with him in it. God intended that Adam learn the joys of dependence, fellowship, diversity, and unity together with someone who complemented or corresponded to him. In fact, that's what the word *meet* means as used in *helpmeet*. In different versions of the Bible this word *meet* is translated "suitable," "comparable," "fit," and "counterpart." In other words, Eve was God's finishing touch for Adam. She, like no other being, completed and harmonized with him. And God gave a wife as a good gift (Genesis 3:12; Proverbs 18:22) to the man.

COMPANION AND HELPER

God made a woman for Adam so that he would not live in solitude, but also so that he would have the help he needed. Of course, this help can include physical labor, but that wasn't the main thrust of her design. Remember that Adam had all the purely physical help he needed in the form of the animals in the garden. If he had wanted to move a tree he didn't need Eve; he had the Behemoth. Also, if the help that God wanted to give Adam was primarily physical, He would have created Eve with more, rather than less, physical strength. No, Eve's helping of Adam was to consist of something beyond mere physical labor, although joyful laboring together with Adam was certainly part of her daily routine.

Fundamentally, a wife can take steps toward helping her husband by seeking to understand the specific ways in which God has called him to rule, relate, reproduce, reflect, rejoice, and rest. Even though we'll look at more tangible ways to help in chapter 3, it would be beneficial for you to begin now to ponder these questions:

- In what specific ways has God called my husband to rule? How can I help him fulfill that calling?

- With whom has he been called to relate? What would helping him in these relationships look like?

- How has God's calling to reproduce been answered in our family? How can I help him with mentoring or nurturing children (physical or spiritual)?

- What does my husband spend time thinking about or reflecting on? How could my help sharpen his thinking or cause it to be more productive?

- What can I do to bring a godly joy into our relationship? How have I failed to help him discover the joy of intimate fellowship?

- How can I facilitate his development of a fruitful rest? What could I do to make our life together a place of harmony and God-centered worship, especially on the Lord's Day?

- What influences could I bring to bear upon him that would help him glorify God and reflect Him more fully?

Perhaps, if you're like me, these questions might seem astonishingly novel. Please don't despair. Even if you've been married for three decades, as I have, you can still begin today to discover God's calling as a helper. You might be thinking, *Yeah, right. My husband is so far from any of those things, Elyse, that I don't think there's any hope for us. Besides, if I asked him any of those questions, he would just shrug and say, "I don't know."* Again, please allow me to encourage you not to despair. Remember that no one is beyond the work of the Holy Spirit and that God may be preparing you to be the means He uses to enliven your husband to God's call on His life.

Although I am growing to delight in the notion of being a helper, that hasn't always been the case. I must admit that in the past, before I began deeply thinking about what this term meant, I thought that being a helper was perhaps beneath me as a woman. Generally speaking, when I heard the term, I tended to think of little toddlers struggling to put their toys away and trying, however inanely, to be "good little helpers." But the concept of being a helper is much richer and far more challenging than I had ever imagined.

GOD IS OUR HELPER

God is *our helper.* Think about that statement. When I place the term *helper* as a descriptor of God's activity and character, it takes on a whole new meaning, doesn't it? I understand that as I grow in my ability to truly help my husband, I'm not regressing into some sort of infantile servitude; I'm becoming more like God: being a helper is one very specific way that women can mirror and glorify the Lord.

When the Bible says that God is our helper, it means that He *protects, aids, succors, supports,* and *surrounds* us. Those are strong, proactive words, aren't they? To *protect* or *aid* is something more than putting away the crayons; to *succor* and *support* are words that depict strength, competence, and a wealth of resources. Of course, no woman (or man) will ever be able to perfectly mirror God's help—He's never late, tired, confused, or in a muddle. His help is perfect; ours is imperfect and weak (at best).

Although we'll never be helpers exactly like God is, let's look at a few passages that speak of His help and see if we can learn about our unique calling.

- "Behold, God is my helper; the Lord is the sustainer of my soul" (Psalm 54:4).

- "Turn to me, and be gracious to me; oh grant Your strength to Your servant. . . . You, O Lord, have helped me and comforted me" (Psalm 86:16–17).

- "Do not fear, for I am with you; do not anxiously look about you, for I am your God. I will strengthen you, surely I will help you, surely I will uphold you with My righteous right hand" (Isaiah 41:10).

- "The Lord helps them and delivers them; He delivers them from the wicked and saves them, because they take refuge in Him" (Psalm 37:40).

- "The Lord is my strength and my shield; my heart trusts in Him, and I am helped" (Psalm 28:7).

In the light of these verses, are you getting a little excited now about what it might mean to be your husband's helper? In a word, then, a wife who is reflecting God's helping character desires to sustain or uphold her husband; she strengthens, comforts, and seeks to protect him. Because of her love for the Lord and for her husband, she endeavors to dispel his fears by being trustworthy and gracious. She leans for strength upon her Lord so that she might share that strength with her husband. In her heart he finds shelter and protection from the world; he finds a companion who offers him what he really needs: help in his God-given calling.

One of the most well-known passages on women is found in Proverbs 31:10–31. Consider these descriptive phrases, found in this chapter, to see what being a helper looks like:

- "The heart of her husband trusts in her, and he will have no lack of gain" (v. 11).

  She's trustworthy, reliable, and always looking for ways to help him become both spiritually and materially productive.

- "She does him good and not evil all the days of her life" (v. 12).

  She's focused on being a help to him and on being a source of good in his life.

- "She . . . works with her hands in delight" (v. 13).

  She finds joy in helping her husband and others through honorable labor.

- "She brings her food from afar . . . and gives food to her household" (vv. 14–15; see also vv. 21–22).

  She helps her husband by freeing him from concern about more mundane matters such as food and clothing; she is conscientious and anticipates the needs of those in her care.

- "She considers a field and buys it; from her earnings she plants a vineyard" (v. 16; see also v. 24).

  She's involved in profitable commerce and oversees business transactions, striving to help her husband financially.

- "She girds herself with strength and makes her arms strong" (v. 17).

  She seeks to become physically, mentally, emotionally, and spiritually strong so that she can be a source of strength and help to him and others, as well.

- "She senses that her gain is good; her lamp does not go out at night" (v. 18).

  She's confident that her life is profitable; she's watchful and protects her family. She helps her husband by encouraging him when he experiences setbacks and discouragements.

- "She extends her hand to the poor, and she stretches out her hands to the needy" (v. 20).

  She sees that others beyond her family need her help, and she's generous with them.

- "She is not afraid of the snow for her household, for all her household are clothed with scarlet" (vv. 21–22).

  She isn't caught off guard; she's discerning of possible future needs and plans for them instead of worrying about them. She helps her husband plan for the future and think with an eternal perspective.

- "Strength and dignity are her clothing, and she smiles at the future" (v. 25).

  She seeks to be a woman of profound moral fiber and worth; she's confident, trusting in God's work in her life.

- "She opens her mouth in wisdom, and the teaching of kindness is on her tongue" (v. 26).

  She's wise and kind and she helps others by sharing these gifts; she speaks the truth in love.

- "She looks well to the ways of her household, and does not eat the bread of idleness" (v. 27).

  She watches over her household and doesn't waste the precious time that her God has granted her.

- She "fears the Lord" (v. 30).

  She helps her husband by controlling sinful fear and worry, and she worships the Lord through obedient, God-glorifying living.

THE HOLY SPIRIT AS HELPER

Let me remind you of another way the title of Helper is used in the New Testament. *Helper* is one of the names used of the Holy Spirit (John 14:16; 15:26; 16:7). This designation is very dear. It is variously translated "counselor," "comforter," "intercessor," "consoler," and "advocate." Again, there are many ways in which our differences from the Spirit are quite obvious, but the thoughts of comforting, consoling, counseling, and interceding are lovely.

How would your husband's life be changed if you spent time focusing on these four endeavors? How would the quality and purpose of your husband's life change if you comforted and consoled him? How would it be better if you gave your counsel to him, instead of holding it back and letting him make his own mistakes? How can you intercede for him with the rest of the family and, most important, with the Lord?

The Greek word for helper, *Paraklētos,* literally means "'called to one's side,' to one's aid . . . and suggests the capability or adaptability for giving aid . . .in the widest sense, it signifies a 'succorer' or 'comforter.'"[4] The Holy Spirit was sent by our heavenly Father to our side: right there, close by, helping, comforting, aiding, and guiding. Isn't it precious that Eve was formed from Adam's side and is called to stay there, adapting herself so that she provides aid, comfort, counsel, and succor?

NEW TESTAMENT WOMEN WHO DISTINGUISHED THEMSELVES AS HELPERS

Another way we can gain an initial understanding of our call as helpers is to look at women who were designated as such in Scripture. Phoebe, a woman who served the church at Cenchrea, is called a helper not only of the church in general, but also of Paul. Paul said of her, "Help her in whatever matter she may have need of you; for she herself has also been a helper of many, and of myself as well" (Romans 16:2).

The Greek word Paul chose to use to describe Phoebe's ministry (*prostatis;* she was a *"helper* of many") is a word rich with dignity and high in esteem. It means that she was regarded as a *protectress* of many people. Think of that. That's why some versions of the Bible translate it "succorer." "*Prostates* was the title of a citizen in Athens, who had the responsibility of seeing to the welfare of resident aliens who were without civic rights."[5] As you can see, our calling as helper is filled with great significance and honor.

Priscilla is another New Testament woman who is spoken of as a helper. She and her husband Aquila are said to be colaborers or fellow helpers of Paul's. At one time, she and Aquila sat down with the great orator, Apollos, and corrected his errant doctrine. Priscilla was a woman who was strong in the Lord. She understood the glorious gospel, knew when she heard preaching that wasn't quite right, and knew how to humbly and respectfully correct it.

ANOTHER HELPER CREATED FROM THE NEW ADAM'S SIDE

As God contemplated the plight of man—his unfavorable solitude, his need for help—He didn't stop at making Eve for Adam. As the Second Adam's Father, God created a beautiful bride for His Son, Jesus, when on Calvary's tree the blood and water poured from His beloved Son's side. This Husband wasn't given the privilege of sleeping through this operation, though, as Adam had. Our Suffering Servant-Leader even refused the offer of gall, a substance which would have deadened the pain and made Him insensible to His suffering. Our great Husband experienced the full effect of taking on our sin and paying the penalty for it—God's fierce wrath.

These truths are even more amazing when we realize that Jesus didn't have any great need for a bride. Christ wasn't alone or in need of help; He'd had joyous fellowship with His Almighty Father for all eternity. The Father's creation of the church as a bride for Christ, is all of grace. He birthed her, made her one with Him, and called her to His side to help Him by serving and being the means through which He completes His Father's will to build a kingdom that will glorify His name forever and display the magnitude of His love.

He's not only opened the way for us to have fellowship with Him, as His bride, He's also broken down the walls of separation between Jew and Gentile, slave and free, educated and uneducated, refined and coarse, rich and poor. God has solved man's need for society by giving us spouses and by placing us all in a worldwide family and then renewing His image in us, so that we each carry the family resemblance. Those who are not married or who are married to unbelievers should seek to become partakers of the joy of intimate fellowship with others through the church, His bride.

The church is called to be this Second Adam's helper by caring for one another through biblical fellowship. The New Testament speaks broadly and deeply about our call to be intensely involved in each other's lives. For instance, we are to comfort (1 Thessalonians 4:18), admonish (Romans 15:14), and strengthen (Hebrews 12:12) each other. Paul directed the Thessalonians to "admonish the unruly, encourage the fainthearted, help the weak, be patient with everyone" (1 Thessalonians 5:14).

We are also called to help carry out the great commission to "Go . . . and make disciples of all the nations . . . teaching them to observe all that I commanded you; and lo, I am with you always, even to the end of the age" (Matthew 28:19–20). Christ promises that we won't be left alone to try to complete any of this work on our own; He promises to be with us forever, solving our great need for help and fellowship with Him, as we submit to His calling.

Are you beginning to see the high calling that God has given you? You're a companion, a helper, and in being these things you are imaging all three members of the Trinitarian Godhead. You're walking in the footsteps of women like Phoebe and Priscilla; you're fulfilling the same roles with which Christ has lovingly commissioned His bride. Being your husband's companion-helper is much more than making his breakfast and sitting with him as he cheers on his favorite football team. It's a holy calling and one that you've been designed to fill, all for your joy and God's glory.

Finding and
Fulfilling Our Calling

1. *What are you learning about God's call to glorify Him by helping your husband? Are you aware of ways in which you have withheld help from him (for whatever reason)?*

2. *Begin to pray specifically about these areas. Pray that God would help you to become a vulnerable and transparent servant. Pray that God would give you understanding into your calling and that you would begin to love it.*

3. *Observe the ways that your husband presently fulfills God's calling in his life and speak to him about it, seeking appropriate opportunities to encourage and bless him.*

4. *Share what you're learning in this book about God's calling in your life and respectfully ask him to pray for you that you would become a better companion-helper. Ask him to give you guidance on ways you could do this as he considers God's call on his life.*

5. *Refuse to be drawn into self-pity, manipulation, or criticism. It's easy to feel sorry for ourselves when we're wishing that we had something other than what we have. Then the next step is to find ourselves angry and manipulative, giving up in frustration or criticism. Even if you perceive that your husband is sinfully uncommunicative, independent, distant, or directionless, seek to overcome evil by being a blessing instead. What would being a blessing look like to the Lord? to your husband?*

6. *Summarize what you learned in this chapter in three or four sentences.*

chapter 3

A Covenant of Companionship

She is your companion and your wife.

∽ MALACHI 2:14

The glistening white coral sand, the embrace of warm ocean waters, and the somnolent gentle lapping of the sea against the shore are typically sensations that evoke thoughts of a visit to paradise. But for Chuck Noland, his surroundings were anything but pleasurable.

Isolated and distressed, Chuck disregarded his powerful company allegiance as he tore open soggy packages the tide had delivered to his deserted island. Videotapes, a pair of ice skates, and a woman's evening gown were each pulled from their boxes, examined, and put aside. In one larger package, a birthday present for a child was found. This gift would, in time, become central to Chuck's survival. The gift? A volleyball.

At first Chuck missed the ball's value, but later, during an attempt to make a fire, he cut his hand and threw the ball in anger. Upon retrieving it, he discovered that his bloody handprint had left an image of a face on its surface. With saliva and a small piece of cloth, he made eyes, a nose, and a mouth. He gave his new friend a name: Wilson.

As the story unfolds, Wilson becomes Chuck's link to normalcy during his exile, as portrayed in the movie *Cast Away*.[1] What I find most interesting about Chuck's story is that it doesn't seem strange for him to name and talk to his volleyball. Why? Because we intuitively know that life without someone in our own image to talk with is not good. Talking to coconut palms or lava rocks just won't do. Chuck needed someone like him, and even though Wilson was a poor representation of another human, at least the trace of a resemblance was there.

Our need for companionship and the evil of isolation are so fundamental to us all that we know how he felt. Being a castaway is not good because existing in isolation is not good. We were created to reflect and glorify God by being in relationships, first with God and secondarily with others.

In previous chapters we've spent time deliberating on the Genesis account without looking at what the rest of the Bible has to say about companionship, although this principle isn't relegated to Genesis alone. This concept of companionship between a husband and wife runs throughout Scripture. Let's look at a few more verses and ask the Holy Spirit to use them to teach us how we can grow as our husband's companion and helper, shall we?

THE WIFE YOU CHERISH

I recall with a sweet fondness how, when I was first married, I discovered the joy of lying with my head on my husband's chest. There, cradled in the bend of his arm, I would listen to his heartbeat and treasure our closeness, the peaceful, steady rhythm of his heart, the comfort that being close to him brought me.

This intimate companionship is illustrated in a phrase crafted by Moses. In Deuteronomy 13:6, he alludes to "the wife of your bosom"

(NKJV). This expression is alternately translated "the wife you cherish" (NASB) and "the wife you love" (NIV). Moses' marriage to his wife, Zipporah, certainly wasn't ideal, but he did recognize the closeness that exists between a husband and wife. She is the cherished one, the beloved, the one who rests in his bosom.

The prophet Micah also uses the same imagery, adding that she is not only the one who "lies in your bosom" but is the trusted one (Micah 7:5 NASB) who influences for both good and ill. What a delightful illustration of intimate companionship! Who could be closer or have more influence in a man's life than she who dwells near his heart?

In warning his son about adultery, this same picture is invoked negatively, "Can a man take fire in his bosom, and his clothes not be burned?" (Proverbs 6:27). Solomon is warning his son that whatever he allows to abide near his heart will greatly influence him.

When you contemplate your relationship with your husband, do you see yourself peacefully lying in the bend of his arm, helping by speaking words of comfort, truth, and strength to him? I know that it's easy to forget, but a wife, because of her nearness, is usually the most powerful human influence in her husband's life. Conversely, when she neglects her calling to direct him toward faithful living, a wife has great potential to harm. This is how David described the heartache caused by an unfaithful friend:

> *For it is not an enemy who reproaches me,*
> *Then I could bear it;*
> *Nor is it one who hates me who has exalted himself against me,*
> *Then I could hide myself from him.*
> *But it is you, a man my equal,*
> *My companion and my familiar friend;*
> *We who had sweet fellowship together.*
> (Psalm 55:12–14)

David's grief was compounded by the fact that the person who was troubling him was his equal, his companion, his familiar friend. This person wasn't just a casual acquaintance; this was a person with whom he had known sweet fellowship, a brother with whom he had an intimate relationship. If David could be so troubled by a relationship breach with one who was merely a friend, how much more are husbands troubled when their wives are false companions?

Let me encourage you now to take these truths to heart and seek to apply them. Prayerfully consider the following questions:

- Do you intentionally seek to be a companion for your husband?

- If an outsider observed your daily routine, would he say that befriending your husband is important to you? How would he be able to tell?

- Are you intentionally setting out to help him by being a continual influence for good in your husband's life? Can you give an example?

- Do you recognize the power that your friendship wields in his life? How do you use that power?

- Have you committed yourself to stand by him throughout all the trials he faces? (In chapter 8, "Because He First Loved Us," I'll provide you with concrete examples of how to do this.)

If these questions (or any that follow) make you uncomfortable, please don't be discouraged. We all have areas of difficulty in our relationships with our husbands, and being a companion and helper isn't something most of us naturally slide into. We all need to grow, and we're not alone in that need. While it is truly a comfort to know that other godly women have walked this path too, it is most comforting to remember that God has promised He will faithfully guide us through all our trials and temptations. Remember Paul's admonition to the Corinthians:

No temptation has overtaken you but such as is common to man; and God is faithful, who will not allow you to be tempted beyond what you are able, but with the temptation will provide the way of escape also, so that you will be able to endure it. (1 Corinthians 10:13)

HE'S NOT HEAVY, HE'S MY HUSBAND

Solomon, too, has something to add to our discussion of companionship. In Ecclesiastes he wrote, "Two are better than one because they have a good return for their labor. For if either of them falls, the one will lift up his companion. But woe to the one who falls when there is not another to lift him up" (Ecclesiastes 4:9–10). In this passage a companion is described not only as a co-laborer but as one who is there to lift his partner up when he falls. Although these verses refer primarily to physical labor, it is also appropriate to view them from the perspective of falling into spiritual or moral failure. Matthew Henry writes, "If a man fall into sin, his friend will help to restore him with the spirit of meekness; if he fall into trouble, his friend will help to comfort him and assuage his grief."[2]

For many a young bride, discovering her husband's imperfection is quite disheartening; that he regularly stumbles and falls is astonishingly distressing! *What happened to that dashing knight who rode in on a white steed to my rescue?* she wonders. *Where did my ideal husband go?*

Adjusting to this reality is one reason why the first five years of marriage often seem so difficult. Many women have spent much of their single lives entertaining vivid imaginations of the bliss that their husbands will bring to them. What a shock it is to learn that their husbands have feet of clay! They stumble! They fall! They sin!

JESUS, FRIEND OF SINNERS

Have you ever considered that God has placed you precisely in the marriage you're in *so that you might learn what it's like to companion and help a fallen one?* He wants us to be conformed to His image—He who was known as the one who ate with "tax collectors and sinners" (Matthew 11:19 NKJV). Why not stop now and meditate on that blessed truth?

> *LORD,*
> *You're the only One who, because of Your purity, has a right to object to a relationship with sinners; and yet, Lord, You're the One who stooped down to befriend me. Help me to remember that it's into Your image that I'm being remade.*

In light of that calling, rather than longing for the day that our husbands change (into our image), we should focus on and pursue our own change into Christ's image. Instead of praying that your husband would change to please you, why not seek to become thankful for God's ability to use even his failures and weaknesses to further your transformation? Of course, we are to pray for and patiently await his growth in holiness, but we must be vigilant to maintain a thankful heart all along the way.

Perhaps this might be a radical thought for some of you, so I'll try to carefully explain what I mean. I don't mean that we should be thankful for our husband's sin itself, as sin is an affront to our Holy God. I do mean, however, that in the midst of our sin-cursed world and relationships, we should be thankful for the way that God uses even sin for His glory and our good. Remember that He causes all things—even our husband's weakness—"to work together for good to those who love God, to those who are called according to His purpose" (Romans 8:28; see also Genesis 50:20).

We're to be thankful that God uses our husband's failures in the same way that He uses our failures in their lives—to glorify Himself and to change us into His image. It's not that we shouldn't grieve over sin, refrain from praying for our husband's sanctification, or withhold respectful confrontation from him when he fails. We aren't called to bury our heads in the sand (or under the pillow), but we are called to befriend and help our dear husband even in his frailty. This is one way that we can learn what it means to share in Christ's sufferings (1 Peter 4:12–13). Of course, His suffering was much greater than ours will ever be simply because He was sinless and we aren't. He's the One who is so pure that He cannot even look on sin (Habakkuk 1:13 niv; see also Job 15:15–16; Psalm 5:4), and He's the One who's known as our friend. Amazing grace!

- Am I willing for God to make me thankful for my husband's failures so that I can learn what it means to be like Christ—a friend of sinners?

Whoa! That's hard, isn't it? It's one thing to be willing to overlook his offenses and failures, but to be *thankful* for them? That's something entirely different! God has called us to a high calling, and for me that's more than just a stretch—it's a Herculean leap. Honestly, I would give up right now in despair if I didn't trust that He will provide grace and strength for me to be my husband's faithful friend. The Lord Jesus has trodden this path before you, and He's there to empower and encourage your walk all along the way. Remember to fix your eyes on Jesus, the "author and perfecter of faith, who for the joy set before Him endured the cross, despising the shame, and has sat down at the right hand of the throne of God" (Hebrews 12:2).

YOU GO FIRST

It's so easy to be deceived about our obedience when we're focusing on someone else's, especially our husband's. It's easy to believe that we would be better at our calling if he were better at his. *If he was being the kind of husband he was called to be, then it would be easy for me to be what I'm called to be,* we think. We have to wrestle with the reality that in thinking in this way we're expecting our husbands to be something that we aren't—sinless—*and we're making our faithful obedience contingent on someone other than Jesus Christ.*

Instead, we need to think deeply about our calling to be a companion and help to a man who is as frail as we. We need to remember that God has called us to help and befriend our husband specifically when he fails; even when he's foolish. The problem that we have to wrestle with is not one of whether our husbands will fail. Our problem lies in our response to that failure. Will we extend a hand of mercy, forgiveness, and tenderhearted help?

GRACE-FILLED RELATIONSHIPS

Recently, in a women's meeting I shared the freedom from legalism into which God had brought me. I articulated how He had called me away from a works-oriented Christianity and toward a grace-filled, peaceful existence with my merciful heavenly Father, who loves me as I am because of His Son. I related my assurance that He was in charge of my sanctification and that He isn't anxious about whether I'm going to make it or not. In some ways I feel like I'm experiencing the comfort that John knew reclining on His loving Savior's bosom (John 13:23).

"The pressure is off for me," I said. "Don't get me wrong, it's not that I'm not pursuing holiness, it's just that I know that my Father will get me where He wants me to be and that even my failures serve, in some way, to glorify Him. My relationship with God is growing to be all about His grace, His mercy, His power."

Joci, a sweet friend, astounded me by responding, "That must be such a blessing for your husband, Elyse. To be walking in that kind of grace must enable you to be so patient and so grace-filled with Phil. To know that God is working in him just as he's working in you must make your marriage so sweet and your husband so pleased. It must be great for him to know that the pressure is off for him, too."

She couldn't have astonished me more if she had jumped up on her chair and hurled a thunderbolt across the room! I loved what she had to say but had to admit that I rarely (if ever) made the connection she made. I scarcely ever extended to Phil the grace I enjoyed with the Lord. Instead, I was frequently more like the man in Jesus' parable who, after he was forgiven a great debt, went out and beat his fellow slave because he owed him some paltry sum. Jesus said, "You wicked slave, I forgave you all that debt because you pleaded with me. Should you not also have had mercy on your fellow slave, in the same way that I had mercy on you?" (Matthew 18:32–33).

I've known these verses and used them in counseling countless times. I'm sure they're not new to you either. But have you ever considered them in light of your marriage? Ponder these questions as you seek to understand this truth:

- Do I consistently have mercy on my earthly husband because my heavenly Husband has had such mercy on me?
- How do I respond to my husband's failures?
- In what ways am I still expecting sinlessness from him?

HIS COVENANT, YOUR COVENANT

In two other passages in the Old Testament this idea of companionship blossoms into clarity with the addition of another word, *covenant.* In Proverbs 2:16–17 Solomon writes of the adulteress who "leaves the companion of her youth and forgets the covenant of her God." The Old Testament prophet Malachi writes about "the wife of your youth [who] is your companion and your wife by covenant" (Malachi 2:14).

In these two verses the imagery of a covenant is invoked. In the first verse the covenant of a woman with her God is noted, whereas in the second the covenant of a man and wife is mentioned. In both places, marriage is to be an unending relationship of companionship.

The word *covenant* is uncommon in our modern vocabulary, so let me briefly refresh your memory. In some ways the ancients used the word *covenant* as we use our word *contract*. A covenant between men was an agreement between two or more parties "in which each party bound himself to fulfill certain conditions and was promised certain advantages."[3]

A covenant is different from a contract, though, in that "a contract always has an end date, while a covenant is a permanent arrangement. Another difference is that a contract generally involves only one part of a person, such as a skill, while a covenant covers a person's total being."[4]

GOD'S COVENANT WITH HIS BRIDE

The Bible speaks of God's entering into covenants with His people, although these covenants are different from covenants between men. In this case, it is always God who initiates the agreement, who makes promises, and who chooses those to whom He will commit Himself. Unlike covenants between men, God never enters into a covenant with mankind because He needs something. He enters into covenants with us because we need something: relationship with Him. Because of His mercy, He delights to give Himself to us. A covenant between God and man binds man together with God into a relationship of commitment. In addition, covenants were always sealed by the shedding of blood; as the covenant with our Father was sealed by the blood of the new covenant, shed by His Son, Jesus Christ (see 1 Corinthians 11:12–26).

One of the most breathtaking covenants of the whole Bible is found in the book of Hosea. This Old Testament prophet was called by God to choose and marry a prostitute to illustrate God's love of Israel, his adulterous wife. God calls to His chosen adulteress and says:

"I will betroth you to me forever. I will betroth you to me in righteousness and in justice, in steadfast love and in mercy. I will betroth you to me in faithfulness. And you shall know the Lord." (Hosea 2:19–20 ESV)

Because of God's mercy, we, God's chosen ones, have been bound to Him in a way that we never could have achieved on our own. Charles Spurgeon writes of this covenant and its effect on us,

> We . . . have passed into a new condition with regard to God. We were once, at the very best, only His subjects, and having sinned we were scarcely fit to be called subjects, but rebels, traitors, attainted of high treason. But now since grace has renewed us we are not only His pardoned subjects, but what is far better, wondrous grace has made us His beloved sons and daughters . . . We are by grace brought into an entirely different relationship from that of fallen nature, and we are ruled and swayed by motives and regulations altogether unknown to the unregenerate sons of men.[5]

As wives, if we have entered into this life-changing covenant with God, we are now "ruled and swayed by motives and regulations altogether unknown" before. By His grace, we're able to be faithful to the covenant we've made with our husbands. Make no mistake about it. You cannot be the kind of companion and helper that God has created you to be without first being renewed by His transforming covenant in your heart. But then, because of His great power, we who have tasted of the mercy of His covenant love are now enabled to flow out with it to our husbands. We now have hope that we will be kept in our covenant commitment to our husbands because of the covenant commitment He's made with us and because now "the love of God has been poured out within our hearts" (Romans 5:5).

We have entered into two life-altering covenants: first with God (as a betrothed wife for His Son), and second, to be a companion to our husband. The first covenant enables us to be faithful to the second, and without this foundational shift, this change of heart, from cold stone to warm flesh (Ezekiel 36:26), we would never succeed.

We will never deal gently with our husband's failures if we haven't first drunk deeply of God's gentleness with us in Christ. We will never deal gently with him if we don't see ourselves as that adulterous bride God lovingly betrothed to Himself.

It is only in the light of this image that we grow in the grace that He's given us. Our covenant with our husband is an agreement, a binding promise to help and befriend him throughout our lives, as God gives us strength. We have committed ourselves to this and God has committed all the resources in heaven to help us be faithful to our agreement.

- How does God's covenant with you impact your relationship with your husband?
- Are you consistently thankful for God's grace? Think of a besetting sin or failing that you have struggled with for years. Rehearse God's patience and gentle dealings with you.
- Do you extend that grace to your husband?
- Do you recognize your covenant as a life-and-death commitment?
- How does the permanence of the relationship influence you?

LIFE ON A DESERT ISLAND

How would you describe your husband's existence? Is he like a castaway or does he know the joy of a close friend? Are you diligently seeking to befriend and companion him? I realize that it's very easy to let the importance of this pursuit fall through the cracks of our hectic lifestyles. Between running the kids to soccer practice, rehearsing for the Easter cantata, and getting to the dentist for our six-month cleaning, befriending your husband might not make it on your "Things to Do Today" list. May I encourage you to begin today to write it there?

I also realize that some women would like nothing better than to be a companion to a husband who keeps them at arm's length. Please don't despair! God can give you the grace to be faithful to your calling, even if you never experience the closeness you're longing for—that's because you're in Him and He has shared in your suffering by befriending sinners and calling them to rest in His bosom. You can find your rest there, too, even if you never find it in your earthly husband's arms.

So wherever you find yourself and your relationship with your one enduring friend, let me encourage you to embrace God's calling and plead with Him to help you grow in His image. He's promised that He will never leave us nor forsake us. He's the One who taught us to say, "The Lord is my helper, I will not be afraid" (Hebrews 13:6).

Finding and Fulfilling Your Calling

1. *Read Jeremiah 31:31–34. Describe God's covenant with His chosen people. In light of His faithful love, how should we respond to our husbands?*

2. *Read 1 Corinthians 10:13. What does God promise you in this verse? How does this promise encourage you, especially when you're tempted to give up in discouragement?*

3. *First Peter 4:12–13 reads: "Beloved, do not be surprised at the fiery ordeal among you, which comes upon you for your testing, as though some strange thing were happening to you; but to the degree that you share the sufferings of Christ, keep on rejoicing, so that also at the revelation of His glory you may rejoice with exultation." Are you enduring a fiery ordeal in trying to companion or help your husband? In what ways are you sharing in the sufferings of Christ? Are you rejoicing as you look forward to the revelation (unveiling) of His glory both here and in heaven?*

4. *In the Old Testament, Ruth makes this covenant commitment to her mother-in-law: "Do not urge me to leave you or turn back from following you; for where you go, I will go, and where you lodge, I will lodge. Your people shall be my people, and your God, my God. Where you die, I will die, and there I will be buried. Thus may the Lord do to me, and worse, if anything but death parts you and me" (Ruth 1:16–17). What are the elements of her covenant? What was she committing herself to do? What is meant by the statement in the last sentence? Do you view your covenant commitment with your husband with that seriousness?*

5. *Although a wife is never called to take the place of Christ in her husband's life, she can be one of the means that the Lord uses to comfort and companion him. Consider the words to the hymn "Jesus! What a Friend for Sinners"[6] to see how He has been your Friend and Help. Remember, it's only as we imbibe deeply of His comfort and companionship that we can extend it to our husbands.*

Jesus! what a Friend for sinners! Jesus! Lover of my soul;
Friends may fail me, foes assail me, He, my Savior, makes me whole.
Jesus! What a Strength in weakness! Let me hide myself in Him;
Tempted, tried and sometimes failing, He, my Strength, my vict'ry wins.
Jesus! What a Help in sorrow! While the billows o'er me roll,
Even when my heart is breaking, He, my Comfort, hears my cry.
Hallelujah! What a Saviour! Hallelujah! What a Friend!
Saving, helping, keeping, loving, He is with me to the end.

Are you your husband's friend, lover, strength, protector, help, and comfort? Do you seek to point him to Christ, His true Friend and Savior?

6. Write out a prayer to the Lord that you would begin to understand and grow in your role as a companion for your husband.

7. In three or four sentences summarize the truths you learned in this chapter.

Father,

Help me to become the companion and lover you have designed me to be for Julian. Help me to grow, even in his failures. Help me to continually point him to You ... to always be his friend, lover, strength, protector, help and comfort. Lord, teach me to love like you.

61

chapter 4

"Here, Dear, Have a Bite"

There is none righteous, not even one . . .
together they have become useless.

∞ ROMANS 3:10, 12

S o far, much of what we've learned in this book has dealt with
God's created order before mankind's ruinous fall into sin. In
this chapter, however, we'll investigate what led up to that fall and
we'll discover how we continue to be impacted by the distortions
that were set in motion then.

A NEW REALITY

Since the tragic events of September 11, 2001, a new govern-
mental position has been created in the United States: the Office of
Homeland Security. The head of this new post has the responsibility
of coordinating national strategy to strengthen protections against
terrorist threats or attacks in the United States. The realities in our
present world have made this office essential, and although we see
the necessity of it, it's a somber turn of events.

AN OLD REALITY

This isn't the first time that a Director of Homeland Security was appointed, however. Actually, the first time someone was charged with the responsibility to protect against terrorist attacks occurred in the Garden of Eden. Let's go to Genesis now and note God's charge to Adam: "Then the Lord God took the man and put him into the garden of Eden to cultivate it and keep it" (Genesis 2:15),

When I read phrases like "cultivate it" and "keep it," I get visions of nicely tended rows of tomato plants. I can picture Adam and Eve, hoeing and weeding, planting the zucchini. Although this phrase does mean that Adam was to care for the garden, its meaning is much broader than simple gardening.

Keep (in the Hebrew *shamar*) actually means "to hedge about (as with thorns), to guard, protect and attend to."[1] God had given Adam the responsibility of protecting the sanctuary where he and his wife lived from attack by a hostile power.[2] In keeping the garden Adam would mirror God, who providentially keeps and guards His people (see also Psalms 25:20; 86:2; 91:11; 116:6; 121:3).

Shamar is also used in another well-known passage, as Cain responded to God's question about his brother's absence. "Where is Abel your brother?" God inquired (Genesis 4:9). Cain replied, "Am I my brother's keeper?" *The Living Bible* paraphrases Cain's retort, "Am I supposed to *keep track of him wherever he goes?*" (italics added). As you can see, the word *shamar* denotes a commitment to protect, manage, and oversee.

Adam was the first Director of Homeland Security, and although he should have been keeping his eye open for intruders and crushing them on sight, he failed in his task, and Eve was left vulnerable.[3] His failure to watch over the garden opened the door for the hostile intrusion of Satan into his home. Once Adam had discovered that an enemy had intruded, he should have driven him out instead of entertaining him.

THE WOEFUL NARRATIVE

We're all familiar with what happened next. Here's the Genesis account:

> *Now the serpent was more crafty than any other beast of the field that the Lord God had made.*
>
> *He said to the woman, "Did God actually say, 'You shall not eat of any tree in the garden'?" And the woman said to the serpent, "We may eat of the fruit of the trees in the garden, but God said, 'You shall not eat of the fruit of the tree that is in the midst of the garden, neither shall you touch it, lest you die.'" But the serpent said to the woman, "You will not surely die. For God knows that when you eat of it your eyes will be opened, and you will be like God, knowing good and evil." So when the woman saw that the tree was good for food, and that it was a delight to the eyes, and that the tree was to be desired to make one wise, she took of its fruit and ate, and she also gave some to her husband who was with her, and he ate.* (Genesis 3:1–6 ESV)

As you can see, both Adam and Eve neglected their calling. Adam failed to keep the garden, the sanctuary of God, free from predators. Eve failed by ignoring her responsibility to help him keep the garden and maintain dominion over the creation (including serpents). Instead of letting the animals influence them, they were to have dominion over them. Their failures would ultimately eventuate in that fateful bite.

Adam and Eve both failed to fulfill their calling, with Adam being more responsible for their ultimate demise, since he was the one who was charged with keeping the garden, the holy place where he met with God, free from wicked intrusion. All of these failures led up to the outward and obvious sin of eating the forbidden fruit. And because they were both able and responsible to obey God, they were both judged. Their fall was all the more heinous because they were created in God's image; it was that precious likeness that was shattered by their disobedience. Although the whole image was seriously distorted by sin, only their original righteousness (found in the spiritual qualities of true knowledge, righteousness, and holiness) was completely lost. Louis Berkhof observed: "It is the moral perfection of the image, which could be, and was, lost by sin."[4]

"YOU WILL BE LIKE GOD"

What was sinful about eating the forbidden fruit? Eating from the Tree of Knowledge of Good and Evil was sinful first of all because it was disobedience. It was also sinful because it implied that Adam and Eve, instead of God, should discern between right and wrong. They set out to construct their own interpretation of morality. Our first parents declared their independence from God's wisdom and sought to center their moral compass on the black hole of man's opinion. In doing so, they tried to usurp God's unique right to differentiate between the clean and the unclean. Only the Lord, in His infinite knowledge, wisdom, and holiness, is qualified to distinguish between good and evil.

How did this newfound "wisdom" serve them? Immediately they became self-aware and decided that nakedness was evil. Their choice resulted in shame and guilt. They then added to their sin by foolishly thinking that they could remedy their plight. They sewed together fig leaves and tried to make themselves acceptable before the Holy God they had just sought to dethrone.

The impact of Adam and Eve's desire to make their own rules is felt even until now. Both husbands and wives seek to determine their own "personal truth" and foolishly strive to live according to it. Even Christians, who recognize absolute truth, must be careful that their code of conduct is biblical and that they aren't adding to or subtracting from His revealed will, but rather, "accurately handling the word of truth" (2 Timothy 2:15) and then bowing before it. That's why we're spending so much time investigating the biblical record: God is the only One who has the authority and wisdom to tell us how to live.

THE FRUIT OF THEIR ACTION

It wasn't long until Adam and Eve were forced to swallow the true fruit of their foolish choice. God walked through the garden in the "cool of the day," and they panicked and hid. So the Lord God called to the man and said, "Where are you?" Adam replied, "I heard the sound of You in the garden, and I was afraid because I was naked; so I hid myself'" (Genesis 3:9).

Although both Adam and Eve were equally culpable for their sin, God addressed His questions directly to the man, who had been charged with overseeing the garden and to whom the command had been given (Genesis 2:16–17). "Who told you that you were naked? Have you eaten from the tree of which I commanded you not to eat?" (Genesis 3:11).

ALL MY SIN IS ALL YOUR FAULT

On a recent vacation my husband and I decided to stop at an ice cream shop for a treat. Instead of getting my normal small fat-free serving, I ordered a large yummy sundae with chocolate sauce, marshmallow cream, vanilla ice cream, and nuts. When I was about three-quarters of the way through, though, I felt sick to my stomach and angry with myself that I had eaten in this foolish way. Instead of owning up to my responsibility in my choices, I teasingly said to Phil, "Why didn't you stop me from eating that thing?" When he just looked at me and smiled, I said, "Don't you know that all my sin is all your fault?" We both chuckled over my question and decided to add it to our repertoire of silly sayings.

Although this vignette was mildly humorous, the realities behind it are deadly. The blame-game has been going on since the first sin was committed in the Garden of Eden. Listen to Adam's reply after He was interrogated by the Lord: "The woman whom You gave to be with me, she gave me from the tree, and I ate" (Genesis

3:12). It is almost as if he said, "The woman You gave to be my helper gave me this. My sin is *Your* fault for giving me such flawed help. After all, I just assumed that she was helping me."

Next, God questions Eve: "'What is this you have done?' And the woman said, 'The serpent deceived me, and I ate'" (Genesis 3:13). Her response insinuated that Adam and the serpent were to blame for her sin. Paraphrased, she said: "It's not *my* fault. If Adam hadn't been sleeping on the job, the serpent wouldn't have gotten in here to deceive me in the first place." Do these responses seem familiar?

PAIN, PUNISHMENT, AND ALIENATION

In response to their monstrous sin, God doled out discipline. He didn't acknowledge their excuses or blame-shifting. He didn't blame Eve for Adam's sin, nor Adam for Eve's sin. Since both of them were created in the image of God, both were obligated and enabled to obey, and both would share in the suffering.

PAIN AND DESIRE

After punishing the serpent, the Lord said to Eve, "I will greatly multiply your pain in childbirth, in pain you will bring forth children; yet your desire will be for your husband, and he will rule over you" (Genesis 3:16). (God didn't get into a discussion with the serpent. God doesn't need to hear from Satan on any account and simply doles out His punishment without paying him the respect of requiring an answer.)

In her created nature as an image-bearer, companion, helper, and nurturer, Eve would be forced to face her folly. She would recognize that, in her quest for godhood, she was the one who had been deceived first. Rather than imaging God through *joyful* procreation, the birth of children (part of her created design) would hereafter be marked by pain, sorrow, and hard labor.

The two words translated "pain" in this passage are first *etseb,* meaning "pain, hurt, toil, sorrow, labor, hardship"; and second, *itstsabown*, which also means "pain, labor, hardship, sorrow, toil" *Itstsabown* is translated in Genesis 3:17 KJV as "sorrow" and as "toil" in Genesis 5:29.[5]

Almost daily, her very physiology would remind her of her frailty and finitude. And she would experience the effect of her sin not only physically but also relationally with her husband. She would be troubled in her rulership with him, and his leadership would chafe her in any one of a thousand different ways, making her role of helper and companion appear abhorrent.

Eve's punishment proves that God looked upon her as equal with Adam in His image. She was just as responsible to know and obey the Law as he was, and she was equally accountable for her actions. She wouldn't be allowed to skirt her obligation with a flippant, "It's my husband's fault. If he had been a better husband, I would have been a better wife."

That God held Eve culpable for her actions, in spite Adam's failure, is significant for us today. Because we've been created (and are being re-created) in God's likeness, we are responsible to walk in faithful obedience no matter what our husbands do or fail to do. I know that seems hard. It's ever so much easier to believe that we would be more compliant if we were married to someone who was perfectly fulfilling his call. Although our husband's godliness does impact us, the power of the gospel is that our obedience is not contingent upon anyone else's, except, of course, that of the Lord Jesus. (We'll look at the ways that our husband's disobedience impacts us and how to respond to it in chapter 11.) At every point of failure in my life, it would be easy for me to say to my husband, "All my sin is all your fault," but that would dishonor Christ and negate the Spirit's power to change my heart—and I would still suffer the consequences of eating too much ice cream. When I think in this foolish way, I'm forgetting God's promise that "greater is He that is in [me] than he that is in the world" (1 John 4:4).

SWEAT, TOIL, AND THORNS

Next, Adam received his discipline.

*"Because you have listened to the voice of your wife, and have eaten
from the tree about which I commanded you, saying, 'You shall not eat
from it';
Cursed is the ground because of you;
In toil you will eat of it all the days of your life.
Both thorns and thistles it shall grow for you;
And you will eat the plants of the field;
By the sweat of your face
You will eat bread,
Till you return to the ground,
Because from it you were taken;
For you are dust, and to dust you shall return."*
(Genesis 3:17–19)

Adam didn't sin because he *listened* to his wife. He sinned because
he harkened to and obeyed her rather than God. God had given him a
command, and rather than obeying the Lord, he obeyed his wife.
Adam's ultimate demise was initiated when he allowed his wife,
instead of God, to be the arbiter of right and wrong (Genesis 3:17).
He was dismissed from his job as caretaker and was forced into a
hard labor, marked by thorns, thistles, sweat, and death. Because of
his sinful eating, the quest to obtain food from a cursed ground
would consume his life. As Solomon wrote, "All a man's labor is for
his mouth and yet the appetite is not satisfied" (Ecclesiastes 6:7).

Consider the tragedy embodied in this punishment, "You are
dust and to dust you shall return." This wasn't just any pile of dust.
No, this was dust who had breathed in the breath of God; dust that
had been uniquely fashioned into the eternal God's image. This was
dust that had been ennobled by God's imprint upon it—dust that
had been given personhood. Instead of enjoying a garden filled with

bounty and beauty, Adam would scratch at the ground from which he had been taken until he was planted in it himself.

A DARK MERCY

But even in Adam and Eve's punishment, God showed mercy. He was merciful by granting them the inevitability of physical death. Death was a mercy because to live on eternally in a sin-riddled and sin-enslaved body would be a horrid punishment indeed; it would be hellish. (In fact, simply put, hell is a permanent state of misery.) In driving the couple from the Garden (and blocking their consumption of the fruit of the Tree of Life), God's kindness was shown. Sin now rules mercilessly over Adam's descendants, you and me, and the realities of living in a sin-cursed world—relational conflicts, confusion, moral failure, crying, misery, slavery, sickness, and pain—are evils that only death releases us from. But even the sting of death is removed from His children as He grants them sinlessness, unhindered fellowship with Him, and access to the Tree of Life (Revelation 22:1–2) in heaven.

Death is a mercy (although frequently a dark one) because death reminds us that Satan is a liar. Those who disobey the Lord and seek their own way will not become a god; they will only discover their neediness. Without the inevitability of physical death we might be deluded into thinking that we are just like the Almighty and that we have the authority and wisdom to devise our own laws.

I'm thankful that the Lord mercifully withheld the immediate annihilation that Adam and Eve deserved. Instead He promised that He would take unto Himself the punishment for their sin and foretold the coming of the Savior, who would reopen the way of life, renew the precious image in us, and clothe us in robes of righteousness.

ADAM'S REPLACEMENT

After Adam and Eve's punishment, they were evicted from the Garden. The Lord "stationed the cherubim and the flaming sword which turned every direction to *guard* the way to the tree of life" (Genesis 3:24, italics added). The word *guard* above is the same word translated "keep" in Genesis 2:15, but where Adam failed, the cherubim wouldn't. Adam had been commanded to guard and keep the garden, but now an angel was put there to keep him out. He had become the profane intruder who was no longer allowed access to the Tree of Life and God's holy presence. How tragic was their sin!

NOT JUST ANCIENT HISTORY

How do these events flesh out in our lives today? Not surprisingly, in many of the same ways. A husband may fail (through apathy, ignorance, or distraction) to guard and diligently watch over his home. He may become sidetracked by work as he sweats and tills the ground, while it yields for him a small crop of useful produce and voluminous bushels of thorns and thistles. Employers deceive, employees beguile, computers crash, stock markets crash, coworkers connive, economies go south—and still the weeds grow.

Our husband may be so busy weed whacking that he forgets the call to image God and keep his garden. He may be tempted to create his own personal code of ethics, while he rationalizes and blame-shifts his disregard for God's law. He may even expect (and sometimes demand) that his wife follow him in this. In myriad ways his God-ordained rule over the home has been corrupted by his sinful heart. He may fail to value and cherish his wife's help. And perhaps he even begins to believe that aloneness would be good, while thoughts of independence seduce him.

Our poor modern Eve is in bad shape as well. To begin with, she finds it natural to militate against her calling as an image-bearing companion and helper. That she was created for her husband

(1 Corinthians 11:8–9), rather than the other way around, tends to be a very bitter fruit. She may also completely disregard her responsibility to help him in his specific calling, as she seeks to carve out a calling more to her own liking, snubbing her God-ordained design. Or she may crown her husband or her children as god, regarding them more highly than she should, creating idols of the family and home. She, too, is tempted to author her own code of conduct, determining what looks right in her own eyes, enticing her husband to follow her word rather than the Lord's. She may even seek to live out her companion-design in relationships with other women, neglecting her husband. (I'm not saying here that women shouldn't have friends. I am saying that women need to be careful that their nature to companion isn't fulfilled primarily in relationships with other women instead of with their husbands.)

This is a pretty bleak picture, isn't it? I don't want you to think that I'm going to leave you here, however, with only this grim perspective, because happily, it isn't the end of the story. As the book progresses, we'll rejoice in God's grace to us as we celebrate His power to refashion us into His image. He knows every struggle we have, and He's faithful to change and enlighten us. But, for now, let's think a little more about how ruling, guarding, and helping have been distorted and especially about those deceptions that look so yummy to us, as wives.

DECEPTIONS IN RULERSHIP

It's pretty obvious to me that the main struggle in our relationships with our husbands is in this area of ruling: both in our calling to rule with them and in their rule over us. When Satan tempted Eve, he wasn't doing so because she was stupid, but rather because he wanted to attack God's designed order, something Satan hates. He enticed Eve to lead Adam, to become more important to him than she should have been; he wanted Adam to worship and obey her, rather than God. He duped her into subverting her role as helper. "Here dear, have a bite" was a perversion of her created nature as a helper who was to assist her husband in serving God. Satan continues to bring confusion about our role as rulers and managers of our garden—the household (1 Timothy 5:14)—all the while seeking to create discontent with God.

- As a woman and a wife, do you find joy in God's order for the family? What do you struggle with the most?
- What has God specifically called your husband to rule over? How focused are you on helping him do that? Do you partner with him in that, seeking his highest good?
- In what ways have you sought to take the place of God in your husband's life, perhaps by expecting him to put you and your desires before faithful obedience to God?
- In what ways have you made your husband your God, perhaps by basing your faithful obedience to God on his obedience or by neglecting God's specific gifting in your life?
- How well are you doing with comanaging and ruling your home with your husband? (1 Timothy 3:4; 5:14) Are you intentionally seeking God's guidance and wisdom in the areas that your husband has delegated to you?

DECEPTIONS IN KEEPING

Our husbands are still responsible to keep, protect, and guard the family. In modeling Christ's love and care for the church (Ephesians 5:22–33), he is to watch over the family and guard it from the deceptive influences of the world, the flesh, and the devil. Again, that's not because women are generally less intelligent or insightful, nor even that they're necessarily more easily deceived. As women we have to wrestle through the reality that God is the One who has the right to assign roles and tasks to His creation, not us. When we think we have a better grasp on what's good for us, we're falling right back into Eve's foolishness.

Modeling the church, which guards the flock against profane intruders, the wife mustn't look the other way when her husband makes a sinful choice or allows ungodly intrusions into her home. She is called to lovingly assist him in keeping the family, acknowledging the implications of the differences between our sinless heavenly Husband, Jesus Christ, and our dear, fallen earthly companion.

- Do you cherish your husband's protection as a gift from God?

- How much thought do you give to helping him in this post? Do you encourage him in it or do you try to find ways around his direction?

- Are you keeping a watchful eye out for intruders that may have sneaked in under the fence?

Deceptions in Helping

I'll admit that, as a woman, it's easy for me to look at a tough situation and assume that I know the best way to fix it. In some ways I can offer real help to my husband, as I bring my perspective, wisdom, and gifts to bear; but in other ways, because of my sinful heart, my help isn't really a blessing. Without much of a stretch, I can see myself acting like Eve, sharing my new recipe for steps toward godhood. I'm like Sarai, helping God and Abram out with the use of my maid, Hagar (Genesis 16). I can work things out like Jezebel, Ahab's wife, eliminating Naboth so that Ahab could have a new garden (1 Kings 21). I can be ambitious enough for both of us, like the disciples' mom who tried to help out their career by suggesting that Jesus consider them for posts of honor on His right hand and His left (Matthew 20:21), although she wouldn't have wanted them by His side as He was lifted up on Golgotha's mount! And I can even tell Phil when it's time to just throw in the towel, like Job's wife did (Job 2:9).

I know that it's hard to discern how much help is helpful and when it's appropriate to step in, isn't it? I frequently find myself swinging back and forth between ignoring his problems (I've got enough of my own!) and trying to manipulate everything in his life by controlling him. I need to make this calling a matter of sincere, heartfelt prayer and diligent study. Do you find that it's the same for you?

- As a woman who's been created to help her husband, how are you doing? Have you focused on this calling? Have you made wisdom about it a matter of earnest prayer? (James 1:5)

- What would God-centered, Spirit-empowered helping look like in your life?

- Do you find yourself trying to control and manipulate circumstances to please yourself, rather than faithfully serving as a helper, to please God?

CURSING INTO BLESSING

In light of God's high calling, we need to drink deeply of the encouragement offered to us in the cross. The promised Messiah, who would crush Satan's head, was born of a woman. Out of the very area of Eve's life that had been cursed for her deceived disobedience would come forth the Savior (Genesis 3:15). She would be saved through childbirth—the birth of a Son would redeem her, carry out God's judgment on her wicked seducer, empower faithful obedience, and guide her into all truth. The words "take and eat" that once spelled disaster and ruin for mankind in the Garden, now speak of comfort and salvation as we gather together at the Lord's Supper. Rejoice with me in His providential gift of a Savior who not only saves us from wrath but also transforms our hearts!

Finding and
Fulfilling Your Calling

1. *Write a job description for your Director of Homeland
   Security. In what practical ways can you help your husband answer this call?*

2. *Access to our Father has been reopened by Christ's death.
   In light of the events in the Garden of Eden, what is the
   implication of the design of the veil that separated the
   Holy of Holies from the rest of the world (Exodus
   26:31–33)? How do the events of Mark 15:37–38
   encourage you?*

3. *Using a Greek study help, do a word study on the words*
   manage *in 1 Timothy 3:4–5,* keep house *in 1 Timothy
   5:14, and* workers at home *in Titus 2:5. What are the differences in these words? What does ruling or managing
   the family look like in your husband's life? What does it
   look like in your life?*

4. *Are there any areas of disagreement between you and
   your husband regarding keeping your home from ungodly
   influence? What are they? How can you help your husband in this area?*

5. *How often do you blame your husband for your failures?
   Do you believe that it is wrong to do so? Why or why not?*

6. *Think about the relationships you have with women. Do
   you have girlfriends that you are closer to than you are
   with your husband? Although friendships are a blessing
   from the Lord, we have to guard against this easy deception.*

God has called wives primarily to help and companion their husband. (We'll look at the problems inherent in our relationships with women in more detail later.)

7. Summarize this chapter with three or four sentences.

chapter 5

What God Has Joined Together

A man leaves his father and mother and is
joined to his wife in such a way that the two
become one person.

∽ GENESIS 2:24 TLB

Wedding celebrations are a fusion of eloquent contrasts. Found in this one ceremony is joy over the anticipation of unexplored love and the envisioning of happinesses yet to be tasted. At the same time, though, marriage marks the cessation of our former lives and relationships, and brings with it the uncertainty and discomfort of a future that will differ significantly from our past. Festivity and solemnity are illustrated in the white of the bride's gown, the black of the tuxedos, the beautiful hues of the flowers and the softly-glowing candles, as two individuals unite to become one. Every facet of the ceremony is designed to make one momentous statement: *two lives are being released from their former mooring and are being joined together into one new person, one new household.*

During the last few years, Phil and I celebrated the marriages of two of our three children. Although we were delighted to do so, I have to admit that the experience was bittersweet. As the day approached for their weddings, I couldn't help but wonder what happened to those giggling little toddlers who screamed with joy when we tickled their tummies. Where did those bare feet, curls, and OshKosh B'Gosh overalls go?

When our children married, I reluctantly recognized that I had to give them the counsel I had given to others. Phil and I had to tell them that they needed to leave us. Ouch, did that ever hurt! We both experienced firsthand the rending of the parent-child relationship, a relationship that we had nurtured and cherished for so many years. Phil wept as he stood at the altar, and I spent months in broken worship, weeping privately before the Lord.

"A man shall leave his father and his mother," Moses wrote (Genesis 2:24). Here, before the fall of man, Moses placed limits on the endurance of all our earthly relationships. Husband and wife, parent and child, each relationship can be summed up in one word: *impermanence.* Think about it: Infants are separated from their mother's womb and then bond to their parents, but before you know it, the little ones are crawling out the door. From the first moment God grants us children, it seems as if they just can't wait to get their balance so that they can stand on their own. And husbands and wives, even those whose commitments last a lifetime, are ultimately separated by death. Wise women recognize these changes as gifts from a loving God's hand.

The undulating transition between leaving and cleaving. . . leaving and cleaving . . . has been fashioned by an all-wise God to remind us that there is only one ultimately unchanging relationship: our relationship with Him. Jesus taught that even marriage, the most lasting of all earthly relationships, will one day be altered: "For when they rise from the dead, they neither marry nor are given in marriage, but are like angels in heaven" (Mark 12:25); while Paul wrote, "The one who joins himself to the Lord is one spirit with Him" (1 Corinthians 6:17). Only our unity and abiding in our heavenly Husband is undying and eternally permanent.

REFLECTING THE SAVIOR

Our triune God is reflected in many ways in the marital relationship, as we have already seen. Here, too, as the husband leaves his father and cleaves to his wife, we glimpse our heavenly Husband. Remember that the Lord Jesus left His Father and His heavenly home (John 3:13) to cleave to His bride, the church. And now all those who have been betrothed to Him have become one with Him, as 1 Corinthians 12:27 says, "You are Christ's body, and individually members of it."

Paul quotes Moses in Ephesians 5, illustrating this correlation between the husband/wife, Christ/church relationship:

> *For the husband is the head of the wife, as Christ also is the head of the church, He Himself being the Savior of the body. . . .we are members of His body. "For this reason a man shall leave his father and mother and shall be joined to his wife, and the two shall become one flesh." This mystery is great; but I am speaking with reference to Christ and the church.* (Ephesians 5:23, 30–32; see also Romans 12:4; 1 Corinthians 10:17; Ephesians 4:15; Colossians 1:18)

A great mystery has been unveiled in the unprecedented relationship between Christ and His church. The unmasked mystery is that human marriages are simply the symbol of a greater reality, that of Christ and His church. God the Father is forming a bride for His Son—a bride made up of people from every nation in the world. The Lord Jesus now thrills over both men and women, Jew and Gentile, and exclaims that we are "bone of His bone and flesh of His flesh!" We have been betrothed to Him in a never-ending spiritual union.

FORSAKING ALL OTHERS

Let's think about traditional wedding vows for a moment. They usually include the promise, "Forsaking all others, I will cleave only to you." Perhaps like me, you normally think about this vow as the pledge of marital fidelity, and while it does mean that, it means much more. Husbands are not only to leave behind or forsake all other love interests, but their own parents, as well. I don't mean that adult children are not to watch over, provide for, honor, and respect their parents, as 1 Timothy 5:4 instructs. What I do mean is that husbands are to leave behind the submission to their parents' authority that marked their childhood. Although parents are frequently a great source of wisdom that wise adult children may seek out, children are no longer obligated to obey them. The relationship has changed significantly, as the husband now seeks to establish a home of his own.

Not only are husbands to leave their parents, but wives are, too, as the psalmist wrote:

> Listen, O daughter, give attention and incline your ear:
> Forget your people and your father's house;
> Then the King will desire your beauty.
> Because He is your Lord, bow down to Him.
> (Psalm 45:10–11)

Although this passage is properly interpreted as speaking of the believer's new allegiance to Christ, the fact still remains that wives are to "forget" their people and their father's house, just as their husbands must. Like Ruth, whom Boaz commended, the wife is to acknowledge that now she has a new people and a new authority in her life. Consider the words he used to bless her:

> "You left your father and your mother and the land of your birth, and came to a people that you did not previously know. May the Lord reward your work, and your wages be full from the Lord, the God of Israel, under whose wings you have come to seek refuge." (Ruth 2:11–12)

"THAT'S NOT THE WAY MY DAD DID IT!"

As a wife, you are now to identify yourself with your husband and his interests, instead of the interests of your childhood family. Leaving is more difficult than simply packing your bags because it involves fighting against yearning for your former, more familiar, comfortable way of life.

This command to leave plays out in a marriage in thousands of seemingly insignificant ways. From dividing up household tasks like taking out the trash (*"In my home that was a man's work!"*) to praying with the children before they fall asleep, we each come into the marriage with preconceived ideas, expectations, and prejudices that have the potential to create significant discord.

Perhaps you grew up in a two-parent home where you experienced a lot of friction with your parents and looked at your marriage as a convenient way out of a bad situation. Or perhaps you thought that you would be able to get along with your husband in ways that you never got along with your parents. Of course, some parents are very hard to get along with, but in my counseling I've discovered that the problems a daughter has with her parents are usually brought into her relationship with her husband. For instance, if you never learned how to resolve conflict biblically or stomped out whenever your didn't get your way, it shouldn't be surprising that slammed doors are part of your new home.

If you never learned to adopt Christ's attitude in your childhood home to "do nothing from selfishness or empty conceit, but with humility of mind regard one another as more important than yourselves; do not merely look out for your own personal interests, but also for the interests of others" (Philippians 2:3–4), then your relationship with your husband will probably be pretty rocky. For you, leaving may also mean abandoning bitterness, unforgiveness, and any other method of manipulation that you used to sinfully get your own way or punish your parents for displeasing you.

Even if you grew up in a fairly stable two-parent home, the truth is that we all have ways of living that we've become accustomed to and expectations of what our husband will do for us. Even if your father was a strong and godly leader, you'll still need to leave him—and the way that he personally lived out his faith and calling—behind. If you had a wonderful relationship with your dad, remember that your husband will always seem less-than, even if he is seeking to be a godly leader, because, of course, he won't have the maturity or wisdom of your much older dad. If you had a difficult relationship with your dad (or no relationship at all), then you'll have to guard against bringing unrealistic expectations, bitterness, and prejudices into your new home.

KNIGHTS IN SHINING ARMOR

For those of you who grew up without a father in the home, the danger of failing in this area is significant, as well. Even though you may have never seen interplay between a mother and father or observed the ways that the workload was divided, you may still have come into your marriage expecting your husband to be everything your absentee father never was. (The unfamiliarity with the true nature of marriage between two fallen people is just one of the many adverse consequences of growing up in a single-parent family.) Perhaps you were shocked by the presence of conflict in your marriage; perhaps you thought that a good marriage meant flowers and romance everyday. Where is that knight in shining armor?

For those who grew up without a father in the home, it's easy to assume that having a man around the house will solve all your problems, from fixing flat tires and leaky faucets to directing your devotion to the Lord. You might think that a father/husband is the one element missing in your life and that being in a relationship with the right sort of man will magically enable you to become the right sort of woman. These deceptions will cause you much heartache and grief (since they are rooted in fantasies instead of the truth). No husband could possibly be everything his wife might desire him to be.

Instead of battling with your husband, hoping to make him into your ideal of your childhood thoughts and dreams, why not fully embrace the husband the Lord has given you and look to Him for your joy, growth, and satisfaction?

I know that it would be easy now for you to think about all the ways that your husband has failed to leave his childhood ways. Please resist that temptation, won't you? Instead, take this time to focus on the areas that you need to improve while you pray for your husband's growth in holiness. For instance:

- Do you compare your husband to your father?

- Do you think that the way you learned to do things is better than the way your husband wants to do them? We each bring into marriage both righteous and sinful ways of living. We need to think carefully about our preferences, discarding the sinful responses while being willing to give up the sound ones for others that your husband prefers. For example, the command to "love your neighbor" is very general and can be lived out in several different ways. Perhaps your parents fulfilled this command primarily by practicing hospitality, but your husband wants to fulfill it by working at a homeless shelter. Both of these activities are godly, and one is not better than the other; what you two choose to do together is merely a matter of preference. The trouble lies in understanding that your preference is not more godly or generally better than his.

- Do you long for your old home and for the comfort and ease of familiarity you had then? When God called Abraham to leave his country, he and Sarah didn't even think of their former country (Hebrews 11:15). How much time do you spend thinking about or longing for your old life?

- Do you respond to your husband in anger when he cramps your style? How did you respond to your father (if you had one in the home) or your mother?

- Are you more concerned about pleasing your mother and father than your husband? Do you become angry with your husband when his decisions don't please your parents?

- Do you speak in ungodly ways to your mother about your husband?

- Have you and your husband made it clear to both sets of parents that you are leaving their authority and establishing a new home?

- If the relationship you had with your parents before you left home was not good, then you need to be sure that you aren't harboring any residual bitterness toward them. If you had trouble resolving conflict or yielding to their authority, perhaps that is also an area of your marriage that you need to work on. Have you confessed this area of sin to your husband? your parents?

- If you didn't have a father while you were growing up, can you pinpoint any ways that you've brought unrealistic expectations into your marriage? Have you spoken to your husband about this?

WHAT GOD HAS JOINED TOGETHER

When Jesus quoted Moses' command to leave and cleave, He added, "What therefore God has joined together, let no man separate" (Matthew 19:6). As God has providentially joined you two together into one, you are to guard against any person who would, for whatever reason, seek to separate you. In light of what we've been discussing, may I paraphrase this verse for you? "Since God has made you two one, don't let your parents or their ways of doing things, separate you." Remember, God's pleasure is more important than your parents'.

You can grow in your calling to be your husband's helper by lovingly encouraging him to leave the former affections of his childhood and by seeking to please him instead of your parents.

A DEVOTED WIFE

Phil and I have what might be considered a strange interest. We like to visit old graveyards and read the epitaphs on the headstones. We love to read the inscriptions, calculate how old the person was when he died, and then imagine the kind of life he might have lived. I think that I can safely say that's not an interest either of us brought into our marriage from our childhood. No, we thought this one up all on our own. We've discovered that one of the more common epitaphs reads, "Devoted Wife and Mother." *What does "devoted wife" mean, I've wondered, and what would being devoted look like in my life?*

In 1 Corinthians 7:33–34, Paul teaches that both the husband and the wife have an obligation to live to please each other: "But one who is married is concerned about the things of the world, how he may please his wife, and his interests are divided. The woman who is . . . married is concerned about the things of the world, how she may please her husband" (1 Corinthians 7:33–34).

Remember that it's both the husband and the wife, as one, who are to leave their parents and seek to be pleasing to their spouse, focusing their energies on this new relationship. Both partners are not only to divest themselves of insisting upon their own personal tastes and customs being respected in the new family; they are to live a life devoted to doing good to their spouse.

Let's look again at Moses' command in Genesis. He wrote, "For this reason a man shall leave his father and his mother, and *be joined* to his wife; and they shall become one flesh" (Genesis 2:24, italics added). Not only are we wives to put off our former relationships with our parents, we are now to be joined to our husbands. The Hebrew word translated "join" in this verse carries the connotation of clinging, sticking with, staying close to, or joining to.[2] "This word yields the noun form for 'glue' and also the more abstract ideas of 'loyalty, devotion'"[3] and affection. In the New Testament, the word *kollaō* is frequently used and means "'to join fast together, to glue, and cement."[3]

In light of the fact that we have left behind the most important relationship of our former life—that with our parents—we are now to "stick like glue" to our husband. This means not only abiding with him in the same proximity, but also includes our devotion. It consists in "uniting . . . so intimately in heart and affection, and at the same time by a bond so indissoluble, that the man and his wife become as it were, one."[4]

A DIVIDED DEVOTION

Just how significant an issue is this cleaving and devotion to our husbands? It is significant enough that it impacts the most important relationship we have—ours with the Lord. Paul teaches that the married woman's devotion is divided between the Lord, whom she is to love preeminently, and her daily concern to please her husband. Paul recognized that we wives "strive to please, to accommodate ourselves to the opinions, desires and interests"[5] of our husbands. Being devoted to them, helping them, loving them, doing them good, and assisting them in fulfilling their calling to serve the Lord is part of what it means to be a helper.

How devoted are you to your husband?

- Where does concern to please your husband fall in your list of priorities for the day? Although our time may be taken up with the family's ancillary interests, such as helping to provide for the home through outside business or caring for the children, does the calling to please *him* have a prominent position?

- How focused are you on accommodating yourself to his interests? For instance, are you willing to spend time at a "boring ball game" so that you can share in what he enjoys? What new skills have you learned so that you might adapt yourself to his favorite pastimes?

- Have you found yourself growing weary of hearing about his daily business, or are you interested and engaged in the pursuits that interest him?

- What are your husband's material and spiritual goals? Have you embraced them as *your own* or are you still pursuing your parent's goals or your personal projects (to the exclusion of his)?

- Your love and devotion to your heavenly Husband is the ground out of which your devotion to your earthly husband will blossom. As you nurture your spiritual life and dedicate yourself to growing closer to Him, you'll find your love and affection growing for your husband. How consistently do you spend time with the Lord in prayer and Bible study? This time of feasting on the daily bread He richly supplies will transform your heart, enlighten your mind, and strengthen your desire to become a woman who pleases her husband.

CLEAVING ONLY TO HIM

We wives are commanded to love, be affectionate to, companion, help, and be bonded to our husband. In my own life, I can see how easy it is to cleave to other people. For me, I think it's most easy for me to cling to my children—and grandchildren. (Want to see a picture?) I also have dear friends that I've bonded with. I have to continually remind myself that the most important relationship I have, after my relationship with the Lord, is the one between Phil and me.

It's easy to be closely committed to our children because, especially when they're young, they love us just as we are. "Mimi, mimi," my little grandson Wesley says. "Can I come to your house?" My heart always melts when he pats my hand, and it's so easy to feel close to him.

It's also easy to cleave to my girlfriends because we're so alike in our designed nature. We love "chick flicks" and chatting about our relationships and difficulties over coffee. My husband, on the other hand, wasn't created primarily as a companion and helper, so if I'm going to achieve oneness with him, I've got to love a nature that is different, in some ways, from my own. Loving my girlfriends is also easier than loving my husband because it's more like loving myself—and they don't ask much of me besides meeting to chat once a week. I'm not called to be one with my kids (or grandkids) or my friends, so in all the places where we disagree, we can just ignore it.

- Do you stay close to your husband? I'm not just talking about staying in the same proximity. I'm talking about staying close mentally and emotionally. Are there barriers or walls between you? Are you both headed in the same general direction? What is that? Do you have the same goals, passions, and love?

- Are you a woman who "stands by her man"? I'm not talking about ignoring his sins or failures. I'm talking about being the one person in the world he can count on to stand by him when everything else is caving in.

- What about the times when he seems to be going in a direction that displeases you? How do you respond?

- Are you loyal to him? What does that loyalty look like?

- Do you see him as the person you've committed yourself to for the rest of your life, or do you think that this is just one of many relationships?

Genesis 2:24 then tells us what will happen when a man and a woman forsake all others to be joined to one another: They become one flesh. Leaving and cleaving *always* results in two becoming one. So, in all the aspects of your life with your husband that you don't feel like you're woven together into one, it will serve you to prayerfully begin to examine how you're doing on leaving and cleaving, clinging to the truth that it's God's power and love that will enable you to fulfill His call.

HIS GOOD GIFTS

God has graciously granted us the opportunity and ability to delight in many varied relationships throughout our lives, hasn't He? He's given us the gifts of parents and children, and sometimes even grandchildren. He's blessed us with friends who enrich and encourage us. He's even placed us in a new family, the church, where we learn to enjoy interdependence and deep fellowship. In all of this He's been exceedingly kind to us.

As wonderful as our friendships and familial relationships are, though, there's only one union that is to permanently endure throughout our earthly journey: the one with our husband. Only that union has the potential to bring us the deep satisfaction and joy that oneness occasions throughout every season, every sunrise and sunset that He grants us together. May our hearts and minds be focused on this oneness as we learn what it means to leave our father and mother and cleave to our husband.

Finding and Fulfilling Your Calling

1. One facet of establishing a new home involves breaking cleanly from your former one. To do this, some counselors suggest writing a letter of thanks to parents that also includes your desire to honor them while setting up a new, independent family structure. Have you ever done anything like that? If not, discuss this possibility with your husband.

2. *What were your expectations of a marital relationship before you married? For instance, did you think that you would have the same kind of relationship that your parents did? Where did you get your ideas about what a good relationship would be like? In what ways have your ideas changed?*

3. *How would you describe your relationship with your father? In what way(s) does the nature of that relationship impact your relationship with your husband? Do you need to confess any sins of anger or rebelliousness? If your relationship with your dad was generally a positive one, how has that impacted your relationship with your husband? Can you see any areas of comparing or dissatisfaction that you need to confess to your husband?*

4. *In what ways has your husband failed to leave his home? Have you made this a matter of prayer? Have you lovingly and respectfully spoken to him about this? (In chapter 10, we'll look at methods of godly communication.)*

5. *What would you say that your husband would write on your headstone (if no one else was going to read it)? Would he write "Devoted Wife"? Why or why not?*

6. *Most women I've spoken with report that they feel alienated from other women. First, I think that there is a specific "Martha Stewart" type of woman that most women assume is the norm and around whom they feel uncomfortable. Do you feel this way? Further, women are never called to be "at one" with another woman, so there will always be a sense of alienation with them. What women are you close to? What is it about them that you enjoy? Are you closer to them than you are to your husband?*

chapter 6

The Two Shall Become One

*In the Lord woman is not independent
of man nor man of woman.*

∽ 1 CORINTHIANS 11:11 RSV

In chapter 5 we looked in depth at the first part of Genesis 2:24, "For this reason a man shall leave his father and his mother, and be joined to his wife." In this chapter, we'll look at the last part of that verse, "and they shall become one flesh."

BECOMING ONE

What does it mean to "become one flesh"? First, and most obviously, becoming one flesh speaks of the marriage act—the joining together of man and wife in sexual union. Since Paul uses this phrase when speaking of illicit relations with a prostitute, we know that a physical oneness occurs through the mere sexual act itself, as in 1 Corinthians 6:16, "Or do you not know that the one who joins himself to a prostitute is one body with her? For He says, 'The two shall become one flesh.'"

So, in the very least, becoming one flesh means just that, and later in this chapter we'll look closely at that facet of oneness. To begin with, though, let's think about the oneness that occurs between a husband and wife aside from their sexual union.

UNITED IN DUTY AND BURDEN BEARING

When a man leaves his parental home and cleaves to his wife, the two become one in many ways. What are some of these ways? Richard Baxter, a Puritan pastor and writer from the 1600s, wrote the following about this pleasurable union: "When husband and wife take pleasure in each other, it uniteth them in duty, it helpeth them with ease to do their work, and bear their burdens; and is not the least part of the comfort of the married state."[1]

Husbands and wives are united in many ways, including their mutual obligations. Aside from the duties that are characteristic only of you two (such as your specific places of employment and fellowship), your preeminent mutual duty is to love God and your neighbor. Because we are one, I want to help Phil in this. I've learned that I can help him love God by speaking the truth in love, by encouraging and comforting him, by praying for him, by helping him see and grow in his areas of weakness, and by setting an example of faithful, God-centered living.

I'm also concerned about what God has commanded him to do specifically as my husband. For instance, the Lord has commanded him to love me "just as Christ also loved the church and gave Himself up for her" (Ephesians 5:25). When I think about that command, all I can do is shake my head in amazement! My heart reaches out in sympathy to him, and I long to help him obey. So, out of love for him and in light of our unified love for Christ, I want to try to make myself easy for him to love. I want to grow past my fickle demandingness and obstinate mulishness so that his sacrifice won't seem so burdensome. I want to be the kind of wife that at the end of our years together he'll say that they "seemed to him but a few days"

(Genesis 29:20).

This doesn't mean that I'll sin to make him happy, or give in to sinful demands just to avoid a confrontation, but rather, in all the ways that it is fit for me to do so, I want to make his obedience to Christ easy. While it's true that it's his obligation to love me, it's also my obligation to help him do so. And since we're one, I want him to excel in his progression toward Christlikeness.

Phil is co-owner of a franchise business that employs around ninety people. Although I am very involved in the ministry that the Lord has called me to, I see that one of my primary obligations is to help ease the burden he bears in the oversight of this business. For us, the oneness that the Lord has called us to encompasses not only our sharing of a home and raising of children and grandchildren but also the God-honoring operation of a company. Oneness means that I seek to be involved in his business, in whatever way I can, rather than saying, "I'm busy with my own stuff." I purposely inquire about areas of trouble, offer counsel and encouragement, and I strive to consistently pray for him. And at whatever level you can, you should seek to do the same—even if all that means is offering a listening ear and consistent prayer.

In like manner, Phil is interested in and supportive of my ministry. He reads all my chapters before I send them off for editing; he listens to my concerns about nuances of theology (and how it plays out in my life), and he diligently prays for me both morning and evening. He loves what God is doing through me and grants me the freedom to pursue His call on my life.

Phil doesn't see my calling as something that concerns only me; rather, he views it as our corporate calling together. Just as it is impossible for me to know everything that goes on in his business, he doesn't need to know all the trivial ins and outs of my day. Even so, we both view one another's calling as our own because, after all, we are one flesh.

UNITY WITHOUT UNIFORMITY

Charles Hodge observed, "The unity of the divine Being; the true and equal divinity of the Father, Son, and Spirit; their distinct personality; and the relation in which they stand to one another, to the Church, and to the world . . . are asserted or assumed over and over from the beginning to the end of the Bible."[2]

Similarly, being one flesh with our husband doesn't mean that we wives should give up God's distinctive calling on our life nor change like a chameleon to mirror our husband. We don't lose ourselves or our individuality; rather, we use our uniqueness to help him. Just as the Father and the Son are one, yet have distinctive callings and personality, so a husband and wife are to be united in common purpose and yet bring their own gifts, perspectives, and strengths to the relationship. (We'll discuss how to finesse the issue of fulfilling God's calling without your husband's support in chapter 9, "Learning the Pattern of the Dance," and in chapter 11, "Helping Your Husband Believe.")

Husbands and wives are also united in burden-bearing. When one has a problem or an affliction, it automatically affects them both, just as it does in the church, where we're commanded to "rejoice with those who rejoice, and weep with those who weep" (Romans 12:15; see also 1 Corinthians 12:26; John 11:35; 2 Corinthians 11:29; Hebrews 13:3). Phil's cares and joys are mine.

- Do you see yourself as "one" with your spouse? Would you describe your relationship more like "two ships passing in the night," "congenial roommates," or a unified cooperation headed towards a common goal? What can you do to make this oneness more intentional?

- How concerned are you to help your husband obey Christ's commands? Do you encourage him in holy pursuits? What could you do that would make it easier for your husband to love you the way that Christ loved the church?

- What gifts has the Lord given to your husband? How can you help him sharpen and deepen them?

GETTING TO KNOW YOU

When a couple first marries, they're usually laboring under a false assumption: They think that they know each other. "We've dated long enough that we've really gotten to know each other," couples often say when they come in for premarital counseling . . . and I try not to laugh. They're all smiles on the wedding day; then the real unveiling begins. It's then that they begin to understand that they didn't really know this person with whom they're sharing everything—at least not as well as they thought they did. "I had no idea that he would leave his socks all over the place!" she moans. "I didn't know she snored like that!" he tries to laugh, as the circles from sleeplessness deepen under his eyes.

These silly, yet revealing, anecdotes (along with others that are not so silly), can be chronicled in every marriage. We all long to be one with a special someone who is bent on knowing us and whom we want to be known by. Then we discover that the special someone we thought was going to fit that bill so perfectly seems to be vegetating in a state of semipermanent unconsciousness, while the person that they really are appears to have been taken over by the Body Snatchers! It's no wonder that most divorces occur within the first few years of marriage, while the Rogers and Hammerstein song "Getting to Know You" takes on a whole new significance.

I think that most women long for a "oneness" with their husbands that might be best described as a "deep knowing." Phil and I have been married for nearly thirty years, and I think I'm finally starting to know him. This "knowing" isn't just a matter of preferences, such as "I know he'll order iced tea now." I think I'm finally beginning to understand how his inner man works—his delights, longings, opinions, fears, and joys.

In order to improve our unity with our husbands, we wives need to be as transparent and vulnerable as possible. I know that this is hard because many women (especially newlyweds) have tried to do this only to be rebuffed by a glazed look and a groggy "Are you talking to me?" Then it's much easier to sinfully hide out, cover up, or respond with a deceptive "nothing" when he asks us what's troubling us. Since we all long for unity with our spouse, though, we need to persevere and by faith open up our hearts and invite him in. In doing so we'll enjoy the oneness that God intended as we experience the knowledge that the pieces of this puzzle fit together just perfectly.

YOUR HUSBAND 101

If you were just meeting me for the first time, what could you tell me about your husband? How would you do on this pop quiz?

1. What does he look like (for those of you who haven't really looked lately)? What size shoe does he wear? What size ring?

2. What part of his anatomy is he most embarrassed about? What would he like to change?

3. Where is he most ticklish? What makes him laugh? What brings him cheer?

4. If he could do anything right now, what would it be? (OK, we'll get to that later.) What else?

5. What does he like about himself? What does he especially like about you?

6. What does he do at work? Whom does he like being with there? Who troubles him? Why?

7. What does he hope to accomplish in his life? for the Lord? for your family?

8. What's the most difficult area of his life right now (besides getting his golf score down or his bowling score up)? Why does this bother him? What does he fear? What makes him angry?

9. What does the future look like for him? Does he face it in faith and confidence? Is he afraid about whom he'll be if he isn't working?

10. How long has it been since you knew the answer to these kinds of questions?

Well, how did you do? It might be tempting right now to say something like, "I've wanted to know him, but he never lets me get near." Please let me encourage you that even if trying to get close to him is difficult, your willingness to try to be one with him is pleasing to the Lord—and who knows when the Lord might move on his heart and open it up for you. Although no one can really plumb the depths of another's heart—in fact, we don't even clearly understand our own hearts, since they are so deceitful (Jeremiah 17:9)—we wives have been called to help and companion our husbands, a task that will be impossible if we aren't growing in our knowledge of them.

- Can you think of anything about yourself that your husband learned only after your marriage?

- Were you open and honest about your goals, desires, thoughts, and loves before your marriage? While we're courting, we all try to put on our best face. Then, once we're married, we feel more freedom to show up without our makeup on. Were there any areas of your life that you purposely concealed from your husband before you were married? Have you spoken to him about this?

- How open have you been since then? If you are harboring bitterness or unforgiveness because of his lack of openness, please take time to confess this to your husband. Tell him that you're pursuing unity in your marriage and that you're going to set the example by sharing your heart with him. Remember that you are the one who is called to help him, so you can't wait for him to take the first step in transparency. Go ahead now and begin to explore him.

- How interested are you in him? It's easy to want to be known, but are you eager to know him? How well do you do asking questions and then listening closely to the answers?

Although there is intimate knowing in marriage, the only One who ever knows us perfectly is the Lord. He is the One before whom our hearts are open and laid bare. He knows us intimately and yet loves us deeply. This is encouraging to us all, but it may be especially so to you if you're married to a man who isn't really all that interested in understanding you. Remember, you can rest in the truth that there is One who knows your heart. You are understood by Him. And once you join Him in heaven, you'll rejoice in being fully known by the Lover of your soul.

THE MOST INTIMATE KNOWLEDGE

It's instructive that the Bible frequently refers to the marriage act in terms of a man knowing his wife. As Wayne Mack writes, "What else can this mean but that *the sex act is a means of deep communion and sharing* through which a husband and wife come to know each other in a very intimate way? . . . *There is no place where this total sharing is more beautifully pictured or fully experienced than in the sexual union of the man and his wife.*"[3]

The sexual relationship is wondrously unique because it is unmasked, unclothed whispers of surrender and intimate self-revelation accompanied by an embracing acceptance of another. It's as though we're saying to our husband, "You see me as I am, and I delight in that; I see you as you are, and I embrace you and am one with you. I surrender myself to you." As the bride in Solomon's Song exulted, "My beloved is mine, and I am his; . . . and his desire is for me" (Song of Songs 2:16; 7:10).

Although our sexual relationship with our husband is meant to bring joy and satisfaction, in my counseling, I've discovered that many women have difficulty in this area. Although this book will not serve as a sex manual, perhaps the next few pages will prove helpful.

IN THE BEDROOM

A woman's struggle in this area usually isn't because she doesn't long for oneness with her husband or doesn't love him or doesn't want to please him. For most (certainly not all), the problem doesn't come from an inability to enjoy sex, but stems from other issues such as lack of interest. For example, I've heard women make statements that go something like this: "My husband is always in the mood, but I'm not. In fact, sex is not usually even on my radar screen! It isn't fair!"

It is true that men and women usually have differing sexual desires, in part due to varying levels of hormones. Men, for instance, produce "about fifteen times more testosterone [the hormone primarily responsible for the sex drive] than women."[4] You can see how men, by their physiological makeup, will normally just have a different interest in sex than women will. For some women, just knowing that their husband isn't a pervert or sex maniac because he's always in the mood, will be helpful.

Women, on the other hand, usually have monthly cycles in which the primary female hormone estrogen and secondly, progesterone, become ascendant and descendent. During the time of the month that you're ovulating (usually from twelve to fourteen days after menstruation begins), it's normal to experience a heightened sexual desire, due to a peak in estrogen production.

In addition to these hormonal differences, the difference in sexual response time for a woman and a man is also significant. While most men are ordinarily "ready to go" in three to five minutes, women usually take much longer—an average of ten to fifteen minutes.[5] (These timetables are not exact and no woman should think that there's "something wrong" if her experience is different.) Even the sex act itself is experienced differently for men and women, with the physical being more intense than the emotional for the man, while the exact opposite is true for most women.

Frankly, these differences have baffled me in the past. I've wondered, *If the Lord wanted us to enjoy our sexuality together, why didn't He make us the same?* Perhaps you've had the same question. As I've grown to understand God's purpose in making us different, yet one, I've come to see His loving hand in this area, too.

MEN AND WOMEN GROWING TOGETHER IN HOLINESS

Since even godly men have a natural desire for sex almost all the time, the Lord uses this strong appetite in a number of ways. First, men are drawn into a committed marital relationship (where they will mirror the Lord and grow in sanctification) because of it. As Paul says, "Because of the temptation to sexual immorality, each man should have his own wife" (1 Corinthians 7:2 ESV). Men who want to live pure lives usually recognize that they need to be married (unless they are gifted for celibacy; see Matthew 19:12; 1 Corinthians 7:32). In marriage, men learn lessons of interdependence and mutual sharing that might pass them by if they weren't married. Marriage also teaches men to learn how to control their natural hungers and prefer their wife—laying down their own desires for her. They learn to depend on her for help other than merely in the area of sex. They also learn to patiently seek the good of their wife before their own.

A woman's sinful bent toward independence is thwarted in marriage, too. Her desire to nurture, help, and be one with a husband

and family is usually only fulfilled in marital interdependence. Because she longs for deep, self-disclosing, other-embracing unity, she learns to put aside comfortable isolation and ultimately to serve her husband in the most personal and intimate area of her being.

For instance, it's easy for me to make a nice lunch for Phil because that doesn't take any vulnerability or self-disclosure. Having sex is different, though, because I must engage my heart and open my innermost being. The Lord uses these challenges to teach me to long for my husband's good, for his growth in holiness, and for his pleasure more than I long for self-protection and autonomy. And, as in other facets of the marriage relationship, our differences also reflect the unity and diversity that are evident in the Godhead. (I don't mean here to infer that God has a body or is sexual. What I mean is that the Lord seems to delight in creating differences between people and then joining them together into one.)

SEX IS GOD'S IDEA

Some women struggle with sex because they wrongly believe that it is "dirty" or "bad." Since the Bible teaches that sex is God's idea, though, wives need to see it as pure and holy. In fact, Proverbs encourages husbands to "rejoice in the wife of your youth. . . . Let her breasts satisfy you at all times; be exhilarated always with her love" (Proverbs 5:18–19). The Hebrew words used in this verse don't mean some lackluster, halfhearted interest. In fact, the word *satisfy* is variously translated "make drunk," "fill," "satiate," and "abundantly satisfy," while the word *exhilarated* means "to be enraptured or intoxicated." Contrary to thinking that sex is dirty, your husband is obeying the Lord's counsel when he drinks deeply of your love.

It is interesting, isn't it, that God could have populated the earth without human involvement and yet chose that children be born through the physical union of a man and his wife? Although fallen mankind has misused this gift of intimate knowledge and oneness and we wives are frequently confused about it, it is important to see that God set up our hearts so that our created desire to be one "does not rest until it again becomes one flesh in the child."[6]

SEX IS MEANT TO BE PLEASURABLE

The Lord could have created our bodies so that sex wasn't pleasurable. But that's not what He's done. Especially for the woman, sex is meant to bring pleasure, and God has designed us uniquely, with bodies that are specifically made to experience enjoyment in the sex act. For example, women have been created with a clitoris, the "only organ in human anatomy whose sole purpose is to receive sexual pleasure."[7] Since God fashioned our bodies in this way, we know that sex is meant to be pleasurable for not only the husband but also his wife. It seems as though, especially in times past, women thought of sex as being only for a man's pleasure—something that needed to be "endured." But that's not the truth. Godly women recognize the Lord's design and rejoice in it.

Because women are meant to enjoy sex (just as men are), it is not wrong for women to initiate it or even plan for it. In 1 Corinthians 7:3–4, Paul makes clear that sex is not a one-way street where the man calls all the shots: "The husband must fulfill his duty to his wife. . . . also the husband does not have authority over his own body, but the wife does." Listen to the way that the bride in Solomon's song plans out a romantic interlude with her man:

> "Come, my beloved, let us go out into the country,
> Let us spend the night in the villages.
> Let us rise early and go to the vineyards;
> Let us see whether the vine has budded
> And its blossoms have opened,
> And whether the pomegranates have bloomed.
> There I will give you my love."
> (Song of Songs 7:11–12, emphasis added)

What do you suppose she had in mind? An agricultural visit? I doubt it. Godly women may and should take the initiative in sexual relations. In fact, if you're a woman who struggles with enjoying sex, taking the initiative will probably help. That's because you'll be able to overcome the feeling that sex is just something that's being done to you.

REFRAINING FROM THE SEXUAL RELATIONSHIP IS SIN

In the passage in 1 Corinthians 7 we quoted earlier, we read, *"Stop depriving one another,* except by agreement for a time, so that you may devote yourselves to prayer, and come together again so that Satan will not tempt you because of your lack of self-control" (v. 5, italics added).

Although most women recognize that they probably don't have sex as much as they should, we rarely think about this abstinence as sin. Yet when we refuse our husband's attentions, we're actually robbing him (that's what *depriving* means in this passage) of what we owe him. In addition to stealing from him what's rightfully his, we're also exposing him and ourselves to unnecessary temptation.

As a wife who's been called to help her husband, this is one of the major ways I can fulfill that calling. If I ignore Phil's needs, then I'm answerable for the storm of temptation with which he has to struggle. If I love him and see that I am one with him in serving the Lord we both love, then I'll seek to keep him from temptation and sin.

SOME REASONS WOMEN STRUGGLE IN THIS AREA

Inability to achieve orgasms. As I stated earlier, this is not a manual about sex, but I don't want to leave this topic without addressing some areas of concern. The Bible doesn't tell me that in order to be a godly, loving wife, I must experience orgasms. I think a lot of women are so focused on doing so that they become frustrated and hopeless when they don't. Achieving orgasm is something many women grow into and is especially difficult if you're worried about how you're performing. For some gals, the unwillingness to release control of their bodies, a sort of false modesty, is difficult as well. I've recommended a couple of books on the topic in the endnotes that might be helpful in the endnotes.[8] Just remember that orgasm isn't necessarily the goal of sex—serving, loving, and helping your husband and treasuring your oneness is.

Guilt over previous sexual sins: premarital sex, extramarital sex, masturbation, abortion. Many women struggle with a healthy sexual relationship because their perspective of it has been so damaged by past sin. For instance, if you used your sexuality to secure a relationship with your husband, it's not surprising that you feel like you're being used now that you're married. Other sins, such as extramarital sex, masturbation, or even abortion, are directly tied to your ability to enjoy sex with your husband. For these, as with all sins, Christ offers forgiveness, hope, and a new beginning. First John 1:9 tells us plainly that if we confess our sins, God will forgive them.

Lustful wandering of the heart and mind. Women who want to have a vibrant sexual relationship with their husband must be wise enough to guard their hearts against the intrusion of any other man—whether that's at work, on the silver screen, or just on the TV at home. If you spend the day watching "soaps," then when your husband gets home he won't look very good to you. If you spend the day reading romance (lust) novels, even "Christian" ones, then your desire to lay down your life and please your husband won't be what it should. These things have the potential to cause dissatisfaction and distract you from your true calling.

Also, you must be careful with your girlfriends to guard the words you speak about your husband, not only because you're called to honor and respect him, but because those thoughts will stick with you when you're with him that evening. Finally, you must be extremely careful not to bond with any other man. This kind of sinful bonding tends to happen a lot in cross-gender counseling, something I strongly oppose. That means that you don't reveal anything about your relationship with your husband or the state of your heart to any man other than your husband, unless your husband is there.[9]

There are many other reasons women struggle in this area, not the least of which is troubles in their marriage relationship, such as in communication and conflict resolution (which we'll look at in chapter 10). Then, of course, particularly when we've been blessed with little children, women are just exhausted by the end of the day and have been longing for some sound sleep more than their husband can possibly imagine. (Is there a sleep-drive hormone?) It's appropriate to communicate your fatigue to your husband, as long as you're doing everything you can to get some rest during the day for him.

HARMONIZING YOUR VOICES TOGETHER INTO ONE

Becoming one is certainly more than having a sexual relationship, and yet it is not less than that. Learning to blend your desires and voice together with your husband to produce God-glorifying praise, even though you're uniquely different, is one goal of your life with him.

The Lord reminds us, even in this, of His great mercy. Not long after Adam and Eve's fall and banishment from the Garden, we read the comforting words, "Now Adam knew Eve his wife, and she conceived and bore Cain, and said, 'I have acquired a man from the Lord'"(Genesis 4:1 NKJV). In light of the tragedy of their sin together, both Adam and Eve were doubtlessly comforted that the human race would continue, even though they had sinned. Life would continue, and through Eve would eventually come the One who would reopen Paradise and place man back in the Garden, in a much better covenant. God can and does redeem our marriages and enables us to reflect His oneness even in this.

Finding and Fulfilling Your Calling

1. The Bible speaks richly about God's knowledge of our hearts. We have been created as people who are social, and we all long to be understood by another. Even if we feel isolated in our family, we can rejoice in the truth that God knows us intimately. See 1 Kings 8:39–40; 1 Chronicles 28:9; Job 34:21, Psalm 139:1–3; Matthew 9:2–4; Mark 2:5; John 1:48; 21:17; Acts 1:24.

2. The Hebrew word for knowing, yaada, is used in a number of ways to indicate intimate and experiential knowledge. It is also generally used to indicate sexual knowledge as in Genesis 4:1, 17, 25; 19:8; 24:16. What do you know about your husband that you learned through your sexual relationship? What have you revealed about yourself to him?

3. If you still have a monthly cycle (you're not menopausal or pregnant), why not plan a romantic interlude on the days that you know you'll be ovulating? (If you don't want to get pregnant, better take some precautions!) How about a trip to the country? Or if that's not doable, why not get one of your friends to baby-sit and put on a little romantic music and candlelight (and nothing else)? I'd be dumbfounded if your husband was disappointed that this wasn't a "spontaneous" burst of love. For those of you who are menopausal, you can try this anytime . . . and you probably don't have to worry about getting a baby-sitter.

4. *Make a copy of the pop quizzes on pages 98 and 99 to take with you on your time together. After you've had a time of enjoying each other's bodies, spend some time exploring his heart and mind.*

5. *If you sinned sexually in the past, remember that the Lord was willing to forgive even David's sin. Pray Psalm 51:1–17. Pray that He would grant you a clean heart and joyful realization of His Spirit working salvation in you. Speak with your husband about your desire to see Christ redeem this area of your life and ask him to pray for you daily and before you have sex.*

6. *A woman can make her love life sing by completing this statement and sharing it with her husband: "I'm not usually in the mood, but you can get me there by . . ." Take time now to prayerfully consider what would help arouse you sexually and then share this information with your husband. (A list of possible "To Help Me Feel Close to You" items may be found in William Cutrer, M.D., and Sandra Glahn,* Sexual Intimacy in Marriage *[Grand Rapids: Kregel, 2001], 263.)*

7. *Summarize this chapter in three or four sentences.*

chapter 7   Called for His Purpose

And we know that God causes all things to work together for good to those who love God, to those who are called according to His purpose.

∞ ROMANS 8:28

If you had followed me down the "hallowed halls" of high school in my junior year, you would probably have caught me humming a catchy little tune with lyrics that went like this:

Me and you, and you and me; no matter how they toss the dice, it has to be,

The only one for me is you and you for me, so happy together!

I can't see me lovin' nobody but you, for all my life;

When you're with me, baby, the skies will be blue, for all my life!

So happy together, How is the weather,

So happy together, We're happy together,

So happy together, Happy together, So happy together, So happy together.[1]

If you're humming the melody to this hit song by The Turtles, then you're as old as I am or you really like the oldies station . . . or perhaps both. In any case, my taste in music in those days wasn't very highbrow, and I really did enjoy the thought of living "so happy together . . . for all my life"! The philosophy of The Turtles really said it for me. . . . Yes, a life of happiness would be mine if I could just find the right "you" for "me."

I'm ashamed to admit that, although I improved on my choice of harmonies and lyrics, my philosophy of personal happiness stayed much the same for many years. I count myself among those many women who go through life looking for that special someone with whom they will be "happy together." Many Christians believe that it's God's desire simply to provide them with someone who will make the sky blue—even when it's pouring rain.

Please don't misunderstand. I'm not saying that there isn't great happiness and joy in marriage because there is and I've experienced it. Nor am I saying that God's answer to the "not-goodness" of Adam's aloneness was flawed. God's good answer to Adam's isolation was marriage, and this relationship can be a great source of happiness and comfort, as I have found in my life. But God's ways are not our ways, and His purposes and goals are as high above ours as the heavens are above the earth (Isaiah 55:8–9); our definition of happiness and His are frequently at odds.

GOD'S PURPOSE IN MARRIAGE

Is it possible to pinpoint one end for all that God has done and continues to do? What was God's purpose in joining two people together in lifelong union? Without being overly simplistic or assuming that I can tap into the secret counsel of the Most High, I can say that I know what God's purpose is (at least generally speaking). *God's purpose is always to glorify Himself.* It is His purpose, in everything He does and commands, to bring glory, praise, and honor to His own Name, as Paul wrote to the Romans, "For from Him and through Him and to Him are all things. To Him be the glory forever. Amen" (Romans 11:36; see question #1 in "Finding and Fulfilling Your Call" at the end of this chapter for more references).

God's purpose in everything He does is to bring praise and honor to Himself. Because His perfections are limitless, the Lord delights in making them known and in teaching us to rejoice in them—all for His glory and praise. So, when we consider God's purpose in creating a woman and in placing her with a man, we have to acknowledge that clearly His first goal is to glorify Himself. Why did God create you as a woman? To bring honor and praise to Himself. Why did God create the marriage covenant? Again, it is to bring glory and honor to Himself—to reveal His perfections to His creation so that we would be happy in Him and praise His Name!

I'm sure that these thoughts are nothing new to you. But now I'm going to speak a little more personally: God's purpose in placing *you specifically* in your marriage is His glory. Whether you believe He simply allowed or actively engineered your marriage, even if you think you made a mistake, God's goal was and is still to glorify Himself—in your marriage!

Before you slam this book down and say something like, "You don't know what's going on in my life!" or "God probably gets glory from others' marriages, but not from mine!" let me explain what I mean. I mean that we tend to have a very limited opinion of what brings God glory: We tend to think that God is only glorified when our lives are nice and tidy, our children well behaved, and our husband a composite of, say, our pastor, William J. Bennet, and Saint

Augustine.

But as I observe people in the Bible whose lives glorified God, that's not what I see. Aside from the Lord Jesus, I see tremendously frail, flawed, sinful men and women whose very struggles glorified God. I'm not saying that we should try to be sinful or have problems so that we can glorify Him (Romans 6:1–2)! No, I'm saying that these things are part of life in this sin-cursed world where God is working everything after the counsel of His own will for the praise of His glory (Ephesians 1:11–12), even though sometimes we don't see how that could happen.

HIS PURPOSE IN *YOUR* MARRIAGE

How does God get glory from our troubles? If you're in a difficult marriage, God is using it in your life to free you from the love of the temporal, to turn your eyes towards Him, and possibly even to fill up the sufferings of Christ (Colossians 1:24). He's teaching you the truth about songs like "Happy Together" and their deceptive philosophies.

I know that when you're in the middle of what seems to be an overwhelming struggle, it's easy to lose sight of these eternal truths. It's at these times that you need to remember that you are not alone. Your Savior is not only there, with you, at the moment of your trial, but those are His footsteps you see on the path before you. He's the One who endured a shameful cross—all for the joy that was set before Him. He clung to the serendipitous truth that soon He would savor the great reward that His Father had for Him—and *by faith you can do the same.* You can rest in His love and the promise of eternal bliss, where you'll fully rejoice in the knowledge that your suffering was not random or trivial. There is an everlasting meaning to all you're going through, and the meaning is that He is, sometimes without our even seeing how, glorifying Himself. But how can this be?

Job's Life

Job is an excellent example of this principle. God brought righteous Job to Satan's attention simply to display His glory. In response, Satan tried to cast doubt on God's goodness by saying that Job only loved Him because God had given him a cushy life. "Let me touch him," Satan snarled. "Then he'll curse you to your face!" The Lord granted Satan's request because lies about God's goodness must be refuted. "Go ahead and touch him," the Lord said. Can you see how God displayed His glory and His Name though Job's life? Can you see how God was more interested in His reputation's being upheld than He was in Job's earthly comfort? Although in the end Job received a great earthly reward, that's not what he's remembered for. He's remembered as a man who glorified God and uttered the words, "Though He slay me, I will hope in Him" (Job 13:15). Why would Job be able to say this? Because God is *that* good and His power works *that* effectually in His children's lives.

The "Great Saints" and You

In the lives of Martin Luther, Corrie ten Boom, and Richard Wurmbrand we see this principle demonstrated clearly. In 1521, after being tried for heresy, Luther was forced to flee for his life and escaped to a castle in Wartburg, where he translated the New Testament into German. I'm sure that he would have rather seen repentance in the leaders of the Catholic church; I'm sure that he thought that his time spent in hiding was a failure and that he wondered at God's providence. How could God use these months when he hid out, disguising his identity?

In the early 1940s Corrie ten Boom and her family were arrested for concealing Jews from the Nazis and were sent to a concentration camp, where her father and dear sister eventually died. Richard Wurmbrand, too, endured months of solitary confinement, years of torture, and constant pain from hunger and cold as he bore the suffering of Christ. His crime? Preaching the gospel to the Romanians. As God used Luther, ten Boom, and Wurmbrand for His glory, ultimate meaning was brought into their sufferings, although they might not have recognized it the moment they lived through it.

The Lord was more interested in the glory that would be afforded Him, as we observe, learn, and delight in His power flowing through distressed lives than He was in their temporal comfort. Countless people were blessed by Luther's work on the New Testament. Due to Luther's translation, a new form of the German language was developed that unified the country. And how many sufferers have been encouraged by Ten Boom's story! Her story of God's strength in the midst of tragedy and His ability to cause forgiveness to flower in a heart is simply marvelous. How many souls have been stricken with love for Christ and inspired to live lives of humble sacrifice by Richard Wurmbrand's scars and battered feet? It's pretty obvious that God is more interested in His glory than our temporal comfort and that He's well able to bring lasting good out of all our trials, even those that seem like they might break us.

As I reflect on the areas of weakness and difficulty in my life that I wish would change, I can also see how God has used these to glorify Himself through me. I admit that my desire to help other women first flowed from problems I was personally facing and for which I needed answers. God used both past and present trials and sorrows in my life to motivate me to study biblical counseling so that others would be blessed and His Name would be glorified.

The Significance of Your Trials

I imagine that you might be confused about the significance of the difficulties you're facing. *How could God use my life, my marriage?* you might be wondering. May I encourage you that we're rarely aware of how He uses us and—recognizing our bent toward pride—that's probably good. I've watched women who suffered with cancer glorify God, and it's been a great blessing for me. I've seen other women suffer in difficult marriages, and breathed in the sweet perfume of Christ's presence, perfume that was given forth through His gentle crushing. May the Lord help us remember how powerful He is and that He's able to bring glory to Himself in the most amazing ways.

HALLOWED BE THY NAME

Is the hallowing of His Name important enough to you that you're willing to suffer for it? It was just that important to Jesus, who is the One who taught us to pray, "Our Father, who art in heaven, Hallowed be Thy Name" (Matthew 6:9 NASB 1978). Now that we've been reborn and are being remade into Christ's image, the driving purpose of our life should be to glorify and exalt our Father. Could you say that the honoring of His Name is that important to you?

HIS GLORY, OUR GOOD

God is re-forming His image in you, a Christian woman. Not only is God glorifying Himself, He is also actively causing genuine good to be developed in our lives. Consider Paul's encouragement to the Romans:

And we know that God causes all things to work together for good to those who love God, to those who are called according to His purpose. For those whom He foreknew, He also predestined to become conformed to the image of His Son, so that He would be the firstborn among many brethren. (Romans 8:28–29)

That Paul said that he knew that "all things" cooperate together under God's providential hand for our good is an astonishing statement. How can it be that the trials we face—the shortcomings and sins we suffer from because of ourselves and others; the tragedies and illnesses we experience—*all* work together for our good? How could Paul make such a broad statement?

117

OUR NEVER-ENDING MAKEOVER

I think it's really fun to get a few of my friends together and go get a makeover, don't you? We giggle and play like we're grown-ups, while a stylist or makeup artist creates a new look. Sometimes we like the new us, and other times we feel like we just need to go wash our faces. Getting makeovers is fun, but it isn't a new concept— God's been doing it for centuries.

God's plan to glorify Himself is accomplished as He works to change you into the image of His Son. Simply put, that's His purpose in putting you in the marriage you're in and that's one of the ultimate rewards you can count on.

Your marriage, its joys, and its troubles are all meant to bring Him glory as they develop Christlikeness in you. Your growth in Christlikeness glorifies His power and wisdom in the same way that your failures magnify His grace—and for those who love Him, displaying these divine qualities are the marrow of their existence.

Christ's sweet character is seen and produced in suffering, trial, and difficulty, as well as in blessing. Your fundamental calling as a woman is to glorify God, and trials are simply the means to that end. The Bible speaks both broadly and deeply about this truth:

- "We also exult in our tribulations, knowing that tribulation brings about perseverance; and perseverance, proven character; and proven character, hope" (Romans 5:3–4).

- "God . . . comforts us in all our affliction so that we will be able to comfort those who are in any affliction with the comfort with which we ourselves are comforted by God" (2 Corinthians 1:3–4).

- "For we do not want you to be unaware, brethren, of our affliction which came to us in Asia, that we were burdened excessively, beyond our strength, so that we despaired even of life; indeed, we had the sentence of death within ourselves so that we would not trust in ourselves, but in God who raises the dead" (2 Corinthians 1:8–9).

- "Consider it all joy, my brethren, when you encounter various trials, knowing that the testing of your faith produces endurance. And let endurance have its perfect result, so that you may be perfect and complete, lacking in nothing" (James 1:2–4).

Take a moment to review those verses. What are we taught about the benefits of trials? We are taught that trials change our character, enable us to comfort others with God's comfort, teach us to trust in Him alone, and make us complete and mature.

DON'T WASTE THIS

Please don't think that God is fickle, putting you in difficult circumstances for some perverse pleasure. No, He's holy, good, and loving—and He loves you and His work in you more than you'll ever know. He knows our happiness and His glory are inextricably bound together and that we'll never be truly happy until we drink deeply of His person and grow in our desire to glorify Him. Consequently, He lovingly arranges our lives to achieve His purpose. Remember that, because He's a loving Father, He'll only allow us to go through the trials that will burn off our dross. Here's a better tune for you to hum instead of "Happy Together":

> How firm a foundation, ye saints of the Lord,
> Is laid for your faith in His excellent Word!
> What more can He say than to you He hath said,
> To you, who unto Jesus for refuge have fled?

"Fear not, I am with thee, O be not dismayed,
For I am thy God, I will still give thee aid;
I'll strengthen thee, help thee, and cause thee to stand,
Upheld by My gracious, omnipotent hand.

"When through the deep waters I call thee to go,
The rivers of sorrow shall not overflow;
For I will be with thee, thy trials to bless,
And sanctify to thee thy deepest distress.

"When through fiery trials thy pathways shall lie,
My grace, all sufficient, shall be thy supply;
The flame shall not hurt thee; I only design
Thy dross to consume, and thy gold to refine.

"The soul that on Jesus has leaned for repose,
I will not, I will not desert to its foes;
That soul, though all hell should endeavor to shake,
I'll never, no never, no never forsake.[2]

Doesn't that hymn encourage you? God is changing you into the image of His Son. He's re-creating in you His image: true knowledge, righteousness, and holiness. He's applying the harmless flame (that sometimes frightens so terribly!) to our souls to consume our sin and refine our nature. He'll never desert us! He's remaking our character and restoring the shattered image. The Spirit is refining us for His glory!

What does the character that He's working in us look like? This work in our lives produces love, joy, peace, patience, kindness, goodness, faithfulness, gentleness, and self-control (see Galatians 5:22–23). The Christlike character produced in us through both trials *and* blessings flows forth from our lives as we experience His gentle, though ostensibly bruising, touch.

Think about the ways that God is causing the character of His Son to grow in you.

- *Self-control.* Do you seek to glorify God by longing for a heart restrained by His love? For instance, God has lovingly blessed us with the gift of communication, but we can abuse and be enslaved by it when we give ourselves to outbursts of anger or words that demean His goodness in ours or our husband's lives.

- *Meekness.* The word *meekness* has lost its meaning in our culture and has become synonymous with being a doormat. Biblically speaking, though, those who are meek view God's dealings with them as good and don't fight, struggle, contend against, dispute, or resist Him. It is not weakness or passivity but rather a "gift of power" that Jesus exercised, not only as He knelt before His Father but also as He stood before Pontius Pilate and the Jewish rulers, when He had all the angels at His command, yet humbly submitted to God's will on the cross. "Described negatively," Vine's Expository Dictionary says, "meekness is the opposite to self-assertiveness and self-interest; it is . . . neither elated nor cast down, simply because it is not occupied with self at all" [3] Do you kick against God's dealings in your life, particularly as it relates to your husband, or are you powerfully submitted to them? Do you trust in God?

- *Faithfulness.* Does the faith you assent to inform your life? Do you really believe that God is holy, good, all-powerful, and wise? The work of the Spirit in your life is to enable you to live in the light of these beliefs, so that those around us, particularly our husbands, will be encouraged in their faith by our steadfast conduct.

- *Goodness.* This refers to an uprightness of soul that abhors evil and loves what is good. It is a heart attitude that shows itself "in a zeal for truth which rebukes, corrects, and chastises, as Christ when He purged the temple."[4] It is a sterner version of kindness. It isn't wimpy, nor is it cross, but it's ready to go to the mat when truth and uprightness are at stake.

- *Kindness.* Kindness is opposed to a harsh, crabby temper. It is easily pleased, "a mildness of temper, calmness of spirit, an unruffled disposition. It sweetens the temper; corrects an irritable disposition; disposes us to make all around us as happy as possible."[5] God is the only one who can tame our hearts and make us into women who are known for their kindness. Is your lifestyle marked with good deeds, expressed in grace and tenderness?

- *Patience.* Patience is the "power to endure without complaint something which is disagreeable."[6] It involves restraint in the expression of one's feelings. Sometimes I forget God's patience with me as I complain and grouse about how I wish the people I love would change more quickly. In practicing patience, we are reflecting God's character, as His anger at sin was restrained by holy love: "Or do you think lightly of the riches of His kindness and tolerance and patience, not knowing that the kindness of God leads you to repentance?" (Romans 2:4; see also 1 Timothy 1:16).

- *Peace.* Because of the gospel, we have peace with God and others. Relationships that know peace have been harmonized or combined so that they fit together without the loss of individual identities. In light of Paul's encouragement to "pursue the things which make for peace and the building up of one another" (Romans 14:19), we wives must put away anemic stabs at peacemaking without true reconciliation and pursue the harmony that flows from a recognition of God's oversight in our lives.

- *Joy.* Joy is an inner character of calm delight whereby we have in view God's goodness and greatness. It isn't mere temporal happiness because we've gotten what we want. Rather, it's a God-centered cheerfulness and happiness that recognizes that His hand is good and that He's placed us in the marriage that we're in for His glory and our endless benefit.

- *Love.* Christian love is charity toward others that is not shown by doing what the person loved desires, but what the one who loves deems as needed by the loved one. It is an unselfish, other-centered frame of heart that seeks to give to the beloved what will eventuate in his greatest good and happiness. But because we'll take a very close look at this kind of love in chapter 8, I'll try to exercise some self-control now and leave you with those simple thoughts.

SO HAPPY GLORIFYING HIM

God's plan is to conform us to the image of Christ and thereby glorify Himself. As I reflect on this truth, it's obvious to me that I need heart surgery. I don't merely need a pacemaker to keep my heart's rhythm straight, I need a transplant! I can see that in many ways I haven't grown past my high-school mentality; I recognize that my default thought pattern is that I would be happy if I had the right persons and possessions in my life, satisfying me. But that's not what the Bible says. No, God teaches me that I'll only be satisfied when I see that the point or end of my life is to glorify Him and enjoy Him eternally. He's my strength and my song! He's my flawless heavenly Father!

I'm rejoicing in the truth that His Spirit is both patient and powerful and that He's committed Himself to completing the work in me that He's begun. I'm celebrating His faithfulness to cause all things—even my trials—to eventuate in His glory and my good. And I'm reveling in the knowledge that, if you're His child, He's obligated Himself to do the same thing for you. Do you feel the same way? Are you excited about His ability to remake you . . . into a woman who fulfills her calling to glorify Him and grow more and more as your husband's helper?

Finding and Fulfilling Your Calling

1. *At the beginning of this chapter I said that everything God does and everything He commands is ultimately for His own glory. John Piper says, "This is why God has done all things, from creation to consummation, for the preservation and display of his glory. All his works are simply the spillover of his infinite exuberance for his own excellence."*[7]

   If the idea that everything God does and everything He commands is ultimately for His own glory is a new idea to you, or if you've never really taken the time to analyze the biblical data about God's interest in His own glory, please see the following verses: Psalm 96:7–8; 115:1; Luke 2:14; Romans 16:27; 1 Corinthians 8:6; Galatians 1:3–5; Ephesians 3:21; Philippians 4:20; Colossians 1:16–17; 1 Timothy 1:17; 6:15–16; 2 Timothy 4:18; Hebrews 13:21; 2 Peter 3:18; Jude 25; Revelation 1:5–6; 4:11; 5:12–13; 19:1, 6–7.

2. *Do you believe that God purposely placed you in the marriage you're in so that you could better glorify Him? How is He glorified in you?*

3. Consider at least two Bible characters who struggled with personal sin and yet glorified God. Who are they? What were their sins? How was God glorified?

4. How can you share in the sufferings of Christ? How is God glorified in your suffering? Review 2 Corinthians 1:5, 1 Peter 4:13; 5:1.

5. God has placed a calling on our lives. What is that calling? Ephesians 4:1–2; Colossians 3:12–13; 2 Thessalonians 2:13–14.

6. In the Old and New Testament, God portrays Himself as the ground and object of the believer's joy. (See Psalm 35:9; 43:4; Isaiah 61:10; Luke 1:47; Romans 5:11; Philippians 3:1; 4:4.) Are you known for your joy? Would your husband say that you rejoice in Christ? What prevents you from doing so?

7. Summarize this chapter in three or four sentences. What truths touched you the most?

chapter 8

Because He First Loved Us

*In this is love, not that we loved God, but
that He loved us and sent His Son to be the
propitiation for our sins.*

∽ 1 JOHN 4:10

J oin with me now as I imagine this situation as it might have
been in heaven. Once, before the beginning of time, there
was a great, honorable, wise, and benevolent king who had a son he
loved immeasurably. "My son," the king said, "I know that you are
happy in my presence and that together we share more joy than has
ever been or will ever be known by any other. We are perfectly content in our companionship with each other and with our servants,
but I would like you to know the joy of being a husband to a bride. I
have chosen out a bride for you and will present her to you as my
gift of love for you. Will you have the bride that I have chosen?"

"Yes, father," the son replied, "I would delight to share our joy
and love with a bride. If it pleases you, I am willing to go and get this
bride and bring her back here, to our majestic palace, to celebrate
our marriage. I'm delighted to think how your honor and greatness
will be displayed to her! I'm joyously contemplating the sound of

your great name being praised in our marriage celebration!"

"My dear son, I will indeed send you to get her. But," the father proceeded gravely, "the bride I have chosen for you is our enemy. Right now she is a rebel against us, son, and she hates us. She has transgressed our holy laws and is awaiting execution. She is not beautiful or loving yet, but we will cleanse and purify her and dress her in garments that befit a queen. Because of my great power and love, she will be gloriously transformed when I am finished with her. She will be the delight of our eyes and will bear our resemblance in her heart. But she is presently a slave in the kingdom of the Hateful One and she loves it there. She is a traitor and despises us. Also, if you go and get her, you will have to pay the penalty for her offenses. You know that I cannot make her ours unless my righteous laws and judgments have been carried out."

The father stopped and looked lovingly into his son's eyes. "Would you bear the judgment that she deserves? Would you uphold our holy reputation and love this one I have chosen for you? Would you love her so much that you would be willing to be emptied and become like her, a slave, and then even be humbled to the point of a shameful death in her place? Will you carry out all my decrees and laws perfectly and still be punished as an evildoer? Will you love my name and our future joy with her this much?"

"How wonderful are all your ways, dear father!" the son exclaimed. "Yes, it will be my joy to know that I am pleasing you in this way. When the time is right, I will delight in this, your will."

"Then I will engrave upon your palms the name of your beloved queen for all time. And although your sacrifice will be great, the joy that we'll have, when your bride joins us here in our home, will make this, your ultimate sacrifice, worthwhile."

CONTEMPLATE HIS LOVE

This story is an allegory of the covenant of redemption. "The covenant of redemption is a mutual compact between the Father and the Son in reference to the salvation of man. . . . The covenant between the Father and the Son was formed in eternity and revealed in time."[1]

How often do you contemplate God's love for you? I don't mean His love for His chosen ones in general—I mean His love for you personally, a woman made (and being remade) in His image. Do you remember that He chose you out before the foundation of the world? Do you see that your name is eternally inscribed upon the palms of His hands? Do you revel in the compelling love that provided what you needed before you were even aware of your needs? I admit that my heart is seldom inflamed to obedience by meditating on these precious truths. I rarely remember His electing love and His Son's unimaginable sacrifice when I have to lay down my life— especially when it comes to my marriage. But in John's first epistle, he makes plain that's the pathway to living as a lover. This love-filled life doesn't start with my contemplating my own goodness or even the goodness of my husband. It begins with my remembering my great need and God's indescribable love—and immersing myself in it.

> *God showed how much He loved us by sending his only Son into this wicked world to bring to us eternal life through his death. In this act we see what real love is: it is not our love for God but his love for us when he sent his Son to satisfy God's anger against our sins.*
>
> *Dear friends, since God loved us as much as that, we surely ought to love each other too.* (1 John 4:9–11 TLB)

Dear sisters, since God loves us so much, surely we ought to love our husbands, John writes to us. I think that it's easy to fulfill the common wifely duties: to keep a house and make dinner, for instance. Even maids and cooks can complete their jobs without ever engaging their heart. But we're called to something higher, more rewarding, but immensely more difficult. We're called to love, and that means more than making a bed or completing a grocery list. It means laying down our lives (John 15:13) and dying to ourselves.

YOUR PASSIONATE LOVE FOR GOD

In His discourse with a Pharisee, the Lord Jesus summarized all the Law. Quoting the Old Testament, He said, "'You shall love the Lord your God with all your heart, and with all your soul, and with all your mind.' This is the great and foremost commandment. The second is like it, 'You shall love your neighbor as yourself'" (Matthew 22:37–39).

Before we look at the kind of love that we're to have for our husbands (our nearest neighbor), let's consider the love that we're to have for God. Jesus said that I was to have a *heart-consuming white-hot passion for my heavenly Father—a love that is so demanding that it makes my love for my husband seem like hatred in comparison* (Luke 14:26)! This love for God is to dominate my thoughts and actions. Every other passion—even my love for my nearest neighbor—must bow before it!

My love for my husband must flow from this enthralling love of God. If my love for him crowds out my love for the Lord, or if I equate my love for my husband with love for God, then I am in jeopardy of making my husband my god. We who are serious about God's directions for wives must be wary of transgressing the first commandment, "You shall have no other gods before Me" (Exodus 20:3).[2] We must avoid idolizing or worshiping our husbands or placing their pleasure and desires before the Lord's. The fact that the *first and greatest commandment* is to love God and the second is to love our neighbor should serve as a caution. The preeminent love in our heart should be wholly devoted to God: He is to be the one with whom our entire heart, soul, mind, and strength is to be enraptured. We are to worship only God and focus our lives on His pleasure; we are to praise and exalt Him alone; we are to live to glorify Him.

LOVE YOUR HUSBAND AS YOU LOVE YOURSELF

The commandment to love God and our neighbor was perfectly fulfilled by our Lord Jesus, whose whole existence is characterized by love, as the hymn writer pens: "Crown Him the Lord of Love! behold His hands and side."[3]

But this command is not only to love God, nor is it merely a command to bake a pie for that person on the other side of the fence. It is a commandment for wives and husbands. No one lives closer to me than my husband. No one is more "my neighbor" than the one I eat dinner with and sleep next to every night. My husband is my neighbor, and I need to love him the way that I love myself.

What does that kind of love look like? *Christian love* is a benevolent frame of mind that results in a choice to do the object of the love good. This kind of love isn't based on any merit in the one loved (see Deuteronomy 7:7–8), nor is it primarily or exclusively a feeling (although it shouldn't be less than that). *Vine's Expository Dictionary of Biblical Words* says, "Christian love . . . is not an impulse from the feelings, it does not always run with the natural inclinations, nor does it spend itself only upon those for whom some affinity is discovered. Christian love seeks the welfare of all (Romans 15:2), and works no ill to any (Romans 13:8, 9, 10)."[4]

The kind of love that we are to have for our husband is a love that asks:

- What does my husband need from me so that he might more completely glorify God in his life? Does he need encouragement or gentle confrontation? Does he need my strength? Does he need my silent prayer? Does he need my counsel and wisdom—or just a back rub?

- What lack is he experiencing that I might fill (without seeking to take God's place in his life or tempting him to idolize me)?

- In this situation, what is the most loving thing for me to do? Should I speak or be silent? Should I act or await God's supply? Do I need to confess my own sins?

- Would he easily recognize that my goal in our relationship (and in this particular situation) is to do him good and inspire him to a life of godliness?

- What would Christlike servanthood look like in this situation? Does he need me to take up the basin and the towel and wash his feet, cleansing him from the defilement of the world (John 13:2–17)? Does he need me to provide a haven of rest and nourishment? How can I best serve him?

- How would I want to be treated? If I were in his shoes, what would beneficent love—love that seeks to do good—look like to me?

- Is my love for him based on his ability to satisfy my desires? Do I think that he's been given to me to rescue me and make my life pleasant, rather than my being given to him to help him?

- How can I love him the way that I love myself?

HALLMARK CARDS AND A BOX OF CHOCOLATES

This kind of love is very different from the love that we see portrayed in the modern media. I get confused when I think about what loving my husband looks like because I've been inculcated by the Western view of love, with its hearts and doilies and Valentine's Day and Hallmark cards. Undoubtedly, romantic love is part of a husband and wife's relationship, but it certainly isn't all there is, nor is it even the majority of what there is. Instead of focusing, as I so frequently do, on Hallmark cards or flowers, I should focus on being my husband's loving neighbor, his companion and helper who seeks to do him good.

Jesus wasn't concerned about people learning to love themselves, nor did He command that we do so. It's quite obvious that He saw that our problem was one of self-love and that we had to focus on loving God and others more. The Lord Jesus defined love as treating others the way that we want to be treated. I am to love my husband the way that I love myself.

In order to fulfill this command, I need to think about the ways in which I love myself. I see that I'm loving myself when I want people to be patient with me, even if it looks like I'm not doing a very good job of changing. I want to be judged by my intentions rather than my actions. I want others to assume the best about me and keep the promises they've made, acting in a trustworthy manner. I long for others who love me enough that they tell me what I need to hear instead of what I want to hear. In these, and in thousands of other ways, I demonstrate that I love myself and know what real love looks like.

- How do you love yourself?
- How do you want to be treated?
- How does this impact the way that you display love for your husband?
- Are you waiting to be loved the way you want to be loved *before* you fulfill Christ's command to love as you love yourself? Do you demand that your husband accept you as you are without any encouragement to change?

LOVE, AS I HAVE LOVED YOU

Not only are we to love our husbands the way that we love ourselves, we are to go a step further. We are to love them the way that our heavenly Husband, Jesus Christ, loves us. "A new commandment I give to you," He said, "that you love one another, even as I have loved you, that you also love one another" (John 13:34). Here we find ourselves mirroring God yet again.

I am to love my husband the way that Jesus Christ, who died for me, has loved me. I am to lay down my life for my husband. I am to spend time meditating on the ways the Lord loves me, and then I am to follow in His footsteps. Let's look at Ephesians 1:3–14 to get a picture of His love:

- He blessed me with every spiritual blessing.
- He chose me before the world was even founded.
- He called me to holiness and blamelessness.
- He predestined me to be adopted as His child.
- The intention of His will was kind.
- He freely bestowed grace on me through our Beloved.
- He redeemed me by the shedding of His blood.
- He forgave my trespasses.
- He revealed His will and kind intentions to me.
- He gave me an inheritance in Him.

What can I say about God's incredible love? This is true love—a love that persistently seeks to do good to the one who is loved. Do I love in the way that He does? Of course not. I can't love exactly like the Lord does because I don't elect people to salvation or redeem them with my shed blood. But I can seek to bless my brother-husband; to stand steadfastly by him in committed relationship throughout our lives; to encourage him to live a godly life and satisfy God's calling; to accept him with grace and personal sacrifice; to be forgiving and open about my struggles; and to assist him in leaving an inheritance for the kingdom that will live on after us.

I can love him in this way because I love my Savior, and by faith, I see His engagement ring on Phil's finger: He's received the Son's ring, He's been chosen and sealed by our Father, and I know that Phil and I will dance together around the throne in the marriage celebration of the ages! In that celebration, I won't be grousing about how much golf he's played nor about whether he's brought me a Hallmark card or fixed the leaking shower. May our hearts be prepared and fit for that kind of joy! May we learn to walk by faith and love our husbands the way that we're loved today!

Are you married to a non-Christian? You can love him in this way, too, because he is made in the image of God, who thrills your heart and soul. Do you see His imprint on your husband's soul? It is right for you to love him, even in his rebellion, because God loved you in your rebellion. You can rest in the truth that you're following in the footsteps of your Lord and uniting with His heart as you reach out to your husband.

Charles Spurgeon reminds us that Jesus Christ also loved his disciples sympathetically:

> He *grieved* with them in their griefs, and *rejoiced* with them in their joys. He *entered into most intimate fellowship* with them in their varied experiences. Let us try to do the same with our brothers and sisters [and husbands] . . . let us *weep* with those that weep, and *rejoice* with those that rejoice. Nothing tends so greatly to oil the wheels of life as a little loving sympathy; let us be always ready with a good supply of it wherever it is needed.[5]

THE GREATEST OF THESE IS LOVE

One of the most exquisite passages in all of literature is found in 1 Corinthians 13, Paul's beautiful illumination of love. Since it's easy to become insensitive to familiar passages of Scripture, I've posed the questions below as a way for you to give yourself a "Love Test."

- I'm more concerned about correct grammar and pronunciation than listening to what my husband says.

- I enjoy being right and knowing the truth more than gently living out the truth.

- I think that having miracle-producing faith is more important than forgiveness and mercy.

- Giving money to my church is more important than spending time with people.

- I rarely complain when I don't get my way and am usually calm rather than disagreeable when my plans fall apart.

- I am gentle and considerate, always looking for an opportunity to do good to others, especially my closest neighbor.

- I'm just as happy when my husband gets time off as I would be if it were I.

- I never talk about my own accomplishments but rather spend time pointing out my husband's and others' achievements.

- I love sharing what I have and don't care if others know that I'm their beneficiary or not.

- I never speak in a rude way to anyone—not even in my heart.

- I don't demand to have things my own way, nor do I think that my own way is always right. I frequently prefer my husband and desire that things go his way. I always pray that God would change me before I concern myself with my husband's faults.

- I'm not irritable and never use my monthly cycle as an excuse for unkind words or actions.

- I don't hold grudges—in fact, I find that people are frequently apologizing to me for offenses I wasn't even aware of.

- I never smirk or say "I told you so" when my husband's foolishness finally comes home to roost.

- I'm always glad when the good and truth prevails, even if it means that I might lose the "moral high ground."

- I'm always faithful to my husband, seeking to display God's
  ^x faithfulness to him.

- I always believe the best about my husband and expect the
  best of him, and always stand my ground in defending him
  against injustice.

So, how did you do? I don't know about you, but I'd rather take one of those fifty-cent "Love Tests" in an arcade and be rated the Last of the Red Hot Lovers! Thank God that He's committed to changing our hearts and replacing our heart of stone with one that can truly love the way He does. I know that this is a high calling. It's much harder than merely making cookies or polishing shoes. It's immensely difficult for me, too. But I trust that the Lord, who loves like this, is able to strengthen me with His grace when I desperately cry out for His help. Remember:

> *We do not have a high priest who cannot sympathize with our weaknesses, but One who has been tempted in all things as we are, yet without sin. Therefore let us draw near with confidence to the throne of grace, so that we may receive mercy and find grace to help in time of need.* (Hebrews 4:15–16)

Draw near to your sympathetic Savior now. Let Him flood you with His helpful grace in your time of need. Your prayer might go something like this:

> *Oh Lord, You who loved me when I was so unworthy; You who laid down Your rights as Eternal God and humbled Yourself to become a man and be confined to a fleshly body; You who were rejected by the very ones You came to save; You who suffered the humiliation and dreadful pain and separation for my sin that You bore on the cross; You alone know what love is! Help me now, for I see in me a great lack and even an apathy about being like You and loving my husband the*

way that You do. Please flood me with Your love and cause me to love him because of You and to be perpetually consumed by thoughts of You and of our wonderful wedding day to come. For Your glory and in Your power I pray, Amen.

THIS IS MY BELOVED, MY FRIEND

The Shulamite woman who described her marriage to King Solomon calls him her *beloved,* her *friend.* Ponder this passage for a moment: "His mouth is full of sweetness. And he is wholly desirable. This is my beloved and this is my friend" (Song of Songs 5:16). Is this how you speak of your husband? Is he your beloved? Your friend? Do you delight in his words? Desire him? Is he your favorite? Your closest friend?

In Titus 2:4, Paul charges the older women to teach younger women to love their husbands. It's interesting that in the Greek of this passage, Paul introduces a new word, *philandros. Philandros* is a combination of two other Greek words, *philos,* which means "friend," and *anēr,* a "man" or "husband." Luke captures something of this term's meaning in Acts 27:3, where he says that Paul was treated with consideration *(philanthropos)* or courtesy or kindness. *Philandros* describes the way you act with fondness or tender affection toward a close friend—and that's how Paul tells wives to treat their husbands.

I find that it's difficult for many women to think about their husbands like this. Women frequently want their husbands to act like their girlfriends, to sit around and chat, to giggle and go shopping for a sleek pair of maroon slides—and when they don't, their girlfriends replace their husbands in their affections. But Paul tells us that we are to act with fondness, affection, and kindness toward our husbands. The Lord doesn't tell us to befriend our husbands if they please us or if they like taking long walks on the beach (something my friends and I love!). No, Paul just gives us a command: "Be affectionate to and befriend your husband." Could I also add, "Be his helper" to that command? It does seem to go together, doesn't it?

YOUR WEDDING INVITATION

Weddings are wonderful. I can't think of any celebration that's more joyous. I recently attended a wedding, and although Camille, the bride, was radiantly beautiful, I enjoyed looking at John's face as she walked through that door. He beamed—and I smiled. A husband receiving and rejoicing in his bride, what pleasure! As I watched John receive Camille and shared in their pleasure, I couldn't help but think of my wedding day—the one nearly thirty years ago—and also of the one to come, when the metaphor of my marriage will be replaced by the reality it was meant to foreshadow.

May I encourage you to keep your wedding invitation before you as you wrestle through the day-to-day life of loving and befriending your husband? Don't worry if you didn't save a copy of your personal invitation; that's not what I mean. If you're the Lord's, then the invitation below is addressed to you personally. (For your pleasure, I've included it in appendix B so that you can make a copy of it to carry with you. Just fill in your name in the blank space.)

To All the Hosts of Heaven,
Cherubim and Seraphim, Rulers and Authorities:
God Most High,
the Father of Glory and Ancient of Days,
joyously announces the marriage of
His Only Begotten Son,
Immanuel,
The Lamb Who was slain and lives again,
Who bears the scars on His hands,
and _____,
who is joined with His Redeemed, Purified, and Perfect Bride.

On a day that has been determined in the counsel rooms of heaven when
she has been fully clothed in His white linen and righteous acts.
The Spirit and the Bride say, "Come—Behold His wisdom! Behold His love!"

Let the one who is thirsty come and join in this celebration for all the ages,
drinking from the crystal clear River of Life and
feasting at the table before His throne.

Rejoice in Our joy and prepare yourself for this day,
You, Our blessed beloved, whom We have chosen and sealed for Ourselves.

Finding and
Fulfilling Your Calling

1. *What does the truth that you were chosen "in Him before the foundation of the world" (Ephesians 1:4) mean to you? Does it impact the love that you have for God? for your husband?*

2. *How does the Bible describe your state before Christ betrothed you to Himself? For help, see Romans 3:9–20; 1 Corinthians 6:9–11; Ephesians 2:1–8; 4:18–19, 22; Colossians 1:21; 3:5–7; Titus 3:3; 1 Peter 1:14; 4:1–3.*

3. *Write a few sentences about God's love for you in light of the above.*

4. *In light of the first and foremost command to love God above all else, can you think of any ways that you might be making a false god of your husband? For instance, are you willing to disobey God in order to get what you want from your husband (or because your husband isn't pleasing you)? Or, do you focus all your existence on his wants and desires without thinking about God's glory and His calling on your life to live for Him?*

5. *How did you do on the "Love Test"? If you didn't prayerfully and soberly consider those statements, please go back to pages 135–137 and do so now. From these responses, pick one or two areas that you are willing to work on and make it a matter of prayer and purposeful planning.*

6. *What would befriending your husband look like in your life? How can you express affectionate consideration to him today? (Think beyond making him his favorite meal or watching football with him, although there is nothing wrong with that.) Are you as open with him as you are with your girlfriends or adult daughters? Are you hiding any secrets or harboring any grievances or bitterness? Have you made a point of making him your friend so that the Word of God won't be open to ridicule? What do you need to do today to begin to change?*

7. *Write a summary of this chapter in three or four sentences.*

c h a p t e r 9 Learning
the Steps
of the
Dance

*But as the church is subject to Christ, so also
the wives ought to be to their husbands in
everything.*

∞ EPHESIANS 5:24

For Christmas this year, my husband gave me a very special gift. He consented to take swing dance lessons with me. You can't imagine what a sacrifice this was for him. Although Phil is very musical and has a wonderful sense of rhythm, moving his feet in set steps at set times was a new experience, to say the least. But because dancing is not as foreign to me as it is to him and because I've always wanted to be able to "cut a rug" when we go to weddings or other special occasions, he lovingly acquiesced.

As we began, our instructors taught the class a pattern of steps that we would have to practice with one another. "One, two, three-and-four, five-and-six," we would all mutter, while trying to perform the turns and changes together. Because we were just learning, the instructors would call out specific steps before we did them. "Basic," they would say, "now, throw out, push-break, and closing basic." I knew what I was supposed to do, but getting my feet to follow my head was a surprisingly difficult problem. Then, we had to change partners every minute or so, and I had to learn how to follow twenty different leads! Each man had a distinct way of interpreting each step and leading. For instance, some didn't lead at all while others practically tore my arm out of its socket when it was time for me to spin around.

By the time I got around to dancing with the instructor, he usually reminded me that I needed to wait for him to lead. Our instructor's wife told the women that we should try to dance with our eyes closed, so that we would have to rely on our partner's lead. This didn't work very well for me. I stepped on the instructor's feet while I blindly stumbled around. "Oops, sorry," I mumbled. He called out for the class to change partners again.

In those first few lessons I learned how difficult it was to let the man lead. My natural tendency to take over when others are fumbling around was exacerbated by the fact that, in this case, I knew what steps we were supposed to be taking. When the instructor called out "side pass" and my partner led an "under-arm pass," I frequently ended up running into him while mumbling my dance mantra, "Oops, sorry."

On the other hand, I loved to watch our instructors dance together. Although they each had distinct steps they could embellish as they pleased—she with a graceful turn of her hand, he striking a masculine stance—they performed as one. Because they had danced together for years and because she knew that it was his place to lead, he was able to do so by applying the very slightest pressure to her hand and she would know just what he wanted. Although she was a very proficient follower, she didn't respond to his lead like a robot, marching lifelessly through each step; instead, she creatively enhanced his lead with movements she initiated on her own. The way that she danced honored her partner's ability to lead. They knew that their goal was to present a single harmonized pattern with nuances of differences that beautified the whole presentation.

THE MARRIAGE DANCE

In some ways, marriage is like a dance. It's an interplay between two different, distinct persons who have decided to move together in a pattern, seeking to develop a lovely oneness and unity. For the Christian, marriage primarily serves as a reflection of the unity between Christ and the church He loves. As the church is to follow the lead of her Savior, her heavenly Husband, so the wife is to follow the lead of her husband, as Paul writes:

Wives, be subject to your own husbands, as to the Lord. For the husband is the head of the wife, as Christ also is the head of the church, He Himself being the Savior of the body. But as the church is subject to Christ, so also the wives ought to be to their husbands in everything. (Ephesians 5:22–24)

In the dance that God has called Christians to, there is no doubt about who should be leading. Quite plainly and in many different texts, wives are encouraged to submit to their husband's lead (see, for example, 1 Corinthians 14:34–35; Colossians 3:18; 1 Timothy 2:11; Titus 2:3–5; 1 Peter 3:1–2). I know that for many women this thought is offensive. A few years ago, I was teaching the course "Marriage and Family Counseling" at a local Bible college when one of the young women asked, "Mrs. Fitz, is there some other word you can use besides *submission?*" I knew just how she felt but had to tell her that *submission* and *subjection* were not my words, they were the Lord's. Submission in the home is not only God's idea but is—as are all the Lord's commands—for our good, our blessing, and our life (Deuteronomy 32:47; 1 Peter 3:10–12).

WHY THIS DANCE IS SO TRICKY

For many women, the idea of submission is difficult because they have misconceptions about it. So before I define what submission and subjection actually mean, I'm going to try to clear up some of those errors.

Submission is not only for wives. The verse before the ones discussed above is "Be subject to one another in the fear of Christ" (Ephesians 5:21). *All Christians,* male and female, are called to humbly and voluntarily subject themselves to each other. In every life context, all Christians are admonished to submit themselves to the authorities God has placed over them:

- Work (Ephesians 6:5–8)
- The family (Ephesians 5:22–6:4; noting that wives are specifically commanded to submit *to their own husbands,* not to all men in general)
- The church (Hebrews 13:17)
- Relations among men in the church (1 Peter 5:5)
- Civic authority (Romans 13:1–5)
- The church's relationship with her Head (Ephesians 5:24)

As you can see, submission is not just something that God slapped on women. Even Jesus Christ willingly submitted Himself to ungodly authorities as part of His ultimate submission to His Father's will (John 19:10–11).

- Do you struggle with submission? Why?
- Do you ever consider Christ's submission to His Father as an example for you to follow?

- Do you delight in watching the church as she obediently submits to Christ? When the church follows other gods (such as wealth, fame, or autonomy) are you grieved?

Submission doesn't mean that you are inferior to your husband. As Paul wrote to the Galatians, "There is neither Jew nor Greek, there is neither slave nor free man, there is neither male nor female; for you are all one in Christ Jesus. . . . you are Abraham's descendants, heirs according to promise" (Galatians 3:28–29).

When it comes to our standing before God, there is no distinction between men and women. As I've repeatedly taught in this book, in essence men and women are the same: We're all equally created in the image of God, equally fallen and in need of salvation. Submission isn't a matter of who is smarter or the most deserving. Submission in marriage is simply another reflection of the beautiful pattern of roles seen in the Trinity. The Son has submitted to the Father throughout all eternity, fulfilling His will, seeking to please Him. When I chafe at the thought of submission, I need to remind myself of the beauty of the Son's submission to His Father. What is more powerful or attractive than the Son's humble prayer, "Not my will but Thine be done"? In the same way, I love to see the church obediently submitting to her Lord. When I think about submission in this context, it becomes winsome and delightful, and I don't grumble foolishly about "fairness" nor sing with the Cowardly Lion, "If I were king of the forest . . ."

- Do you ever question God's wisdom in making your husband your leader? Have you thought about the implications of questioning God's design?

- Is your submission winsome and patterned after Christ's? When you're tempted to resist your husband's leadership, do you wrestle with your heart through Spirit-empowered prayer?

- Although Jesus had legions of angels at His disposal, He made God's will His will and set aside the power He possessed. You probably have significant power over your husband to demand your own way or punish him when he displeases you. Do you willingly surrender this power so that he can lead you with a gentle touch?

Submission doesn't mean that you give in to the sinful demands of your husband. The Bible is filled with numerous examples of godly men and women who disobeyed established authority when that authority overstepped its bounds. God has granted a certain authority to every human institution: the family, the church, and the state. God has also set limits to this authority: *No one has the authority to command anyone else to sin or to compromise his conscience.* (We'll look more deeply at this principle in chapter 11, "Helping Your Husband Believe.") When the apostles were strictly commanded by the religious authorities to stop witnessing for Christ, they said, "We must obey God rather than men" (Acts 5:29). God has set your husband as the head of your home, but his headship isn't unlimited—your submission is "as unto the Lord." In every case where your husband seeks to follow Christ and lead you to greater love and service for God, you are to follow him, but if he tries to turn you from the Lord or asks you to join him in sin, you are to respectfully and humbly refuse.

- Are you willing to stand for the Lord even when it might mean difficulty in your home? It's frequently easier to give in to a husband's sinful demands than respectfully refuse. At heart, it's a matter of priorities. Whose approval—God's or your husband's—are you seeking? Are you willing to suffer for righteousness' sake?

- What would respectful refusal look like in your marriage? Do you know how to continue to act in a respectful manner while refusing to submit to sin?

- Sometimes a wife must simply refuse to continue to support her husband in some sinful lifestyle. For instance, if he asks you to call his work and say that he is sick when he's hungover from a binge the night before, you must refuse. The questions that you must always ask yourself are these: (1) What action would most clearly glorify God? (2) What would devoutly loving my husband in this situation look like?

Submission doesn't mean always agreeing with everything your husband does. Because our husbands are both finite and fallen, they make mistakes. Sometimes they simply forget what the next steps are supposed to be; at other times they're distracted and step all over your feet. Sometimes they think they're making a great decision and it turns out to be disastrous. One of the ways God has called you to help your husband is to lovingly offer him your perspective. As we've seen over and over, it isn't good for him to be alone; he needs your insight, as Proverbs 27:9–10a teaches: "Oil and perfume make the heart glad, so a man's counsel is sweet to his friend. Do not forsake your own friend." In the same way that a nice lotion makes your dry hands feel better, your respectful counsel to your husband is a pleasant gift to him.

If, after you've clearly given your perspective and prayerfully presented your point of view, your husband continues on a course that you disagree with but which isn't sinful, you are obligated to support and obey him. In the meantime, you can pray that God changes your heart (or your husband's) and that He would use this circumstance in your lives to draw you both closer to Him and each other.

- Women tend to worry and be afraid about the consequences of their husband's decisions. During these times it's good to encourage yourself about God's sovereign rule over all His people. I love the truth that even if Phil makes wrong decisions, God's will is still being accomplished and He will cause all things to work together for His glory and our ultimate good. How do you react when your husband makes a decision that you disapprove of? Do you recognize the possibility that your perspective may be wrong?

- Do you offer sweet and respectful counsel to your husband? Or do you angrily clam up and just wait for him to fail? Have you ever spoken the dreaded words, "I told you so!"? Is your counsel like "oil and perfume," making your husband's heart glad that he has such a wise, bold, and loving wife?

- Do you continuously seek to influence your husband through thoughtful persuasion and private prayer? Remember that even if your husband refuses to hear your counsel, your heavenly Father's ear is always open to your cry and He has promised to meet with you and reward you with Himself as you seek Him in prayer.

- Do you trust that God is able to use your husband's mistakes for His glory and your good? The Bible boldly teaches that God sovereignly rules over man's decisions (Proverbs 16:1, 9; 20:24; 21:1; Daniel 4:35) and that man is responsible (Ecclesiastes 12:14; Romans 2:16; Jude 1:14–15; Revelation 20:12). Even though your husband is responsible for his decisions, good and bad, you can rest in the reality that God is sovereignly ruling over your life to bring you into the image of Christ and glorify Himself.

Submission doesn't mean that you put your husband in the place of Christ. The first commandment, "You shall have no other gods before Me" (Exodus 20:3), is to impact every facet of your life, even your relationship with your husband. In light of our desire to be loving, compliant wives, we must guard against making an idol of our husbands or our marriages. Our primary allegiance should always be God-centered; *the worship of our hearts must belong to Him alone.* As I've said, Jesus directed us about exclusivity in our worship. "If anyone comes to Me," He taught, "and does not hate his own father and mother and wife and children and brothers and sisters, yes, and even his own life, he cannot be My disciple" (Luke 14:26). In saying this Jesus didn't mean that we are to hate our family per se, but rather that in comparison to the love, worship, and devotion we have for Him, our devotion to them should seem like hatred.[1]

I am not to worship my husband, nor am I look to him as my primary source of spiritual strength or growth. The Bible is clear that our worship belongs only to God and that we must focus our entire existence, love, and trust on Him alone. Your husband is not to be your god; instead, he has been given to you to help you serve the true God, as you have been given to him.

- In what ways have you made your husband a god? For instance, do you expect him to broker your spirituality? Do you pray even if he doesn't? Do you study the Scriptures even if he refuses to do so? Do you expect him to be your savior and solve all your problems, spiritual or otherwise? Do you see yourself as personally responsible before God? Do you expect him to make you disciplined, gracious, loving, joyful, or generous?

- Do you look to him to satisfy the longing in your heart that can only be filled with God? The heart that has been created for intimacy with God will only be satisfied by an intimate relationship with Him. Your husband was not created to satisfy you in this way, and depending upon him to do so is both idolatrous before God and unfair to him.

- If your husband is struggling spiritually, do you seek to strengthen, comfort, encourage, and stimulate him, or do you think since he's the leader that's his role alone?

WHAT SUBMISSION IS

Now that we've cleared up some possible misconceptions, let's look at what submission actually entails. First of all, the Greek word for *subjection* or *submission* is *hupotassō,* a word that means "to arrange under, to subordinate, to subject oneself, to obey, to submit to one's control, to yield to one's admonition or advice."[2] The term is used forty times in the New Testament in reference to familial, civic, and ecclesiastical and spiritual government.

For instance, Jesus submitted Himself to His earthly parents, demons were subjected to the disciples' and Christ's authority, the creation was (and is) subjected to futility because of sin, and all things will ultimately be subjected to the Lord's rule (Luke 2:51; 10:17, 20; Romans 8:7, 20; 10:3; 13:1, 5; 1 Corinthians 14:32, 34; 15:27, 28; 16:16; Ephesians 1:22; 5:21–22, 24; Philippians 3:21; Colossians 3:18; Titus 2:5, 9; 3:1; Hebrews 2:5, 8; 12:9; James 4:7; 1 Peter 2:13, 18; 3:1, 5, 22; 5:5).

Submission to your husband flows out of your sincere, faith-filled submission to the Lord. On your own, you won't be able (or willing) to submit to your husband's leadership. In fact, since the Fall, all of Eve's daughters have militated against submission. In part, that's due to God's judgment on Eve for stepping out of God's established order when she obeyed the Serpent instead of her husband (and the Lord).

The order established by God at Creation (before the Fall) was God ruling over man, who was to rule over the woman, who together were to rule over the animals. In the Fall, this order was turned on its head! In Genesis 3 we find an animal ruling over a woman, who rules over her man, who seeks to usurp God—the right order between the husband and the wife is reversed. In Genesis 2:25 we read of "the man and his wife," whereas in 3:6 we find, "the woman . . . and her husband."

Following the Fall, God decreed: "Your desire will be for your husband" (Genesis 3:16). Although the meaning of this phrase is somewhat ambiguous in Hebrew, it is clear that Eve's desire will be to dominate her husband. The Hebrew word for "desire" here is also used in Genesis 4:7, where it is sin that desires to master Cain. "The picture is of a desire to dominate, which must either conquer or be conquered. In other words, the battle of the sexes is a result of the Fall."[3]

The judgment is not the fact that we must now submit to our husband's leadership, for as we have just seen, the order established was established in the Garden *before* the Fall. The judgment is that there are now problems in this relationship, whereas before the Fall Eve joyfully and willingly submitted. She probably didn't even think about "submission" per se, as Adam lovingly served and led her.

In addition to this very specific judgment on women, all sinners are filled with self-will and pride. It is our self-will—our prideful belief that our way is best, united with our distrust in God's love and wisdom—that causes us to resist our husbands and the Lord. In light of the realities of our heart, it is apparent that our first step in learning to submit to our husbands is to humbly submit to the Lord, for "'God is opposed to the proud, but gives grace to the humble.' Submit therefore to God" (James 4:6–7, referring to Psalm 138:6 and Proverbs 3:34).

We all desperately need God's grace. We require His strength, without which we'll fail miserably. But this strength isn't available unless we first humble ourselves by submitting wholeheartedly to His good will. Until we humbly say to God (and mean), "You're wise, You're loving, You're all-powerful, and Your way is right," we'll never have the power (or desire) to submit to our husbands' leadership, and our obedience to them will be lifeless drudgery at best. Before you can embrace the creative, enlightened, and willing submission you've been called to, you must answer one heart-stopping question: *Have you been purchased by Christ as His bride?* If so, then you're His, and you (and I) no longer have the right to choose how we'll live or whose will we will follow. Once this question is genuinely settled, then God will enable us to embrace and grow in submission to our husband.

Can you see how your faithful submission to your husband is actually a submission to the Lord Jesus, your heavenly Husband, who loves you more than you can possibly imagine? He protects, provides, and satisfies you, and it is He who stands behind your husband when you bow your heart before his will, submitting "as to the Lord" (Ephesians 5:22). Just knowing that it's really my sweet Savior I'm submitting to helps me, while at the same time it also convicts me of my hard-heartedness.

Submission is an embracing of the mission and vision of your husband. *Hupotassō,* the Greek word for "submission," is a "military term meaning 'to arrange troop divisions in a military fashion under the command of a leader.' In non-military use, it [is] 'a voluntary attitude of giving in, cooperating, assuming responsibility, and carrying a burden.'"4 Just as soldiers in an army make the battle plan of their commander their own, so you are to embrace the mission, calling, and vision of your husband, making it your own. You are to bring all your gifts and strengths to him for his use, as he fulfills God's calling in his life. In this way, submission is much deeper than mere obedience, although it is not less than that.

Our submission is to be patterned after the church's submission, as Paul teaches. The church is to embrace the call to glorify God on earth by building His kingdom in myriad ways. All churches are called upon to fulfill Christ's general commands, but specific churches are gifted to excel in specific areas. In the same way, we wives are to embrace God's specific call on our husbands' lives and make it our lives' goal to help them in it. Rebecca Jones writes, "The church is to adopt Christ's heart,"5 as we are to adopt our husband's heart.

- Specifically, what is your husband's calling? How can you adopt his heart in his calling? Philippians 2:4 admonishes us, "Do not merely look out for your own personal interests, but also for the interests of others." It's very easy for me to think that ministry to women, particularly in counseling and writing, is the most important work there is. That's because my gifting and interests lie there. This verse, and the general admonition to subject myself to my husband as the church does, teaches me that my own interests are not to take precedence over my husband's interests. I am to value his interests as more important than my own (Philippians 2:3).

Submission is both voluntary and mandatory. Let's face it. No one can force you to submit your heart to your husband, any more than you could be forced to dance a waltz with style and creativity. It may be possible to force someone to comply to certain demands when threatened, but the kind of submission that Christ is looking for from you only comes voluntarily, through trust in God's providential care. Our Lord calls to us and says,

> *In this, you will be like Me in a very precious way, daughters. You will learn to submit the way that I submit to my Father. Do you long to be like Me? Then walk in My footsteps and you will learn the great joy of obedient submission under My Father's loving hand.*

Even though our submission is voluntary, it is also mandatory. As wives, it's important for us to see that submission has implications that reach far beyond the borders of our homes. We're acting out a priceless and unique dance when we submit: we're demonstrating before all of creation—people, angels, and powers—the astounding interplay between the members of the Godhead. As the Son submits to the Father, and the Holy Spirit submits to the Father and the Son, so our submission as wives mirrors the order in the Trinity.

In chapter 7 we learned that God's preeminent purpose in all He does is to glorify Himself. God's purpose in ordering the family as He has is to glorify Himself by portraying His hidden nature through our roles—*and that's what's at stake.* Of course, God displays His character and glorifies Himself in many ways, and He's glorious enough that He doesn't need my obedience per se. But I must see that my submission is something more than whether I'll acquiesce to my husband's desire for beige carpet or his desire for me to iron his clothes for Sunday morning. Our submission is about God and His glory and the disclosing of His nature to both the visible and invisible worlds. So, is your submission mandatory? Yes. You've been commanded to submit. But you also need to see the reality behind the command—*we're talking about God's glory here.*

- You've been given the high privilege of reflecting something of His winsome nature to the world. Will you joyfully consent? Will you see the One who is standing as Master behind your husband? Will you ask Him to open your eyes to the impact of your obedient submission on your husband, your children, your extended family and friends, and even on the angels?

- Have you asked Him to give you a desire to glorify Him through your submission?

- In what specific areas of your relationship do you find submission particularly difficult? Why?

As you can see, submission is a spiritual issue. It's not just an issue of mere outward obedience. It's an issue of your heart, and your success or failure in this area reflects deeply your heart's spiritual condition. Do you trust Him? Are you willing to obey? Will you cease from demanding your own rights and willingly say, "Not my will but Thine be done," to your Father?

Wayne Grudem writes: "Submission is an inner quality of gentleness that affirms the leadership of the husband."[6] Think about the kind of gentleness that affirms your husband's leadership. In the New Testament, the adjective *gentle,* as used in describing Sarah's submission (1 Peter 3:1–6), is twice used of Christ, and has a very interesting definition. "It means 'not insistent on one's own rights,' or 'not pushy, not selfishly assertive,' 'not demanding one's own way.'"[7] So then, in every circumstance (except when obedience is sinful), you are to reflect the nature of your Lord Jesus by laying down your rights as He did:

Have this attitude in yourselves which was also in Christ Jesus, who, although He existed in the form of God, did not regard equality with God a thing to be grasped, but emptied Himself, taking the form of a bond-servant, and being made in the likeness of men. Being found in appearance as a man, He humbled Himself by becoming obedient to the point of death, even death on a cross. (Philippians 2:5–8)

- What are your rights? What would laying down your perceived rights look like?

- Do you insist on your own way? Are you pushy or self-assertive? Are you demanding?

- Would your husband say that you're a gentlewoman? Would he say that you affirm his leadership? Do you look for opportunities to honor his leadership? Cultivate an atmosphere where his input is not only acceptable but desired? Are you regularly asking your husband for his counsel? Do you believe that God can lead you through him?

- Do you have Christ's attitude? He taught, "A slave is not greater than his master, nor is one who is sent greater than the one who sent him" (John 13:16). At heart, do you believe that you ought to have rights that the Son of God declined?

TOGETHER IN THE DANCE

Phil and I have enjoyed learning to dance together—not just during the past few months but also for nearly thirty years. I'd like to say that I've become proficient at following him, but instead I frequently find myself mumbling "Oops, sorry" after I've tromped all over his feet. I also know that frequently he's tried to lead me in a certain dance pattern while I've insisted on another —only to find out later that he was correct about the rhythm and the steps.

You know, there's a great difference between the type of dance you do with a partner and the dances I grew up doing—which you could do alone if you liked! The awkward gyrations and hopping around that passed for dance when I was young (and still does) is really an appalling illustration of the independence and autonomous individuality that many husbands and wives bring into marriage. When the music begins, we discover ourselves out on the dance floor of our lives with a partner whose movements may or may not have anything to do with our own. (Why, we don't really even need to know what they're doing, so long as we stay out of one another's way!) The problems start when the demands of life press us together in such a way that one of the partners must lead, make decisions, plot the next step or pick the music, and the other must follow. That's when the actual state of our hearts is revealed and many dancers think it's time to move on to a new partner—or teach our present partner how to dance the way we prefer.

I'll admit that I'm probably more proficient and practiced at movements that display self-will and pride. If it weren't that I was confident in my Lord's ability to refashion my heart, I would despair. I know that the Lord is meek and gentle, though, and I know that He can reform me into His image. He can grant us all the strength, wisdom, and true humility we need. He can teach us the steps and tune our ears to hear the music He's playing, while He gently and lovingly leads us, because He is, after all, the Master of the Dance.

Finding and Fulfilling Your Calling

1. *Is your submission empowered by the Holy Spirit? What would that look like?*

2. *The following verses demonstrate the godliness of disobedience to ungodly authority: Exodus 1:17; Daniel 3:16–18; 6:10; Hosea 5:11; Matthew 22:21; Acts 4:19–20; 5:29; Hebrews 11:23. What were the circumstances that occasioned this disobedience? Are there any*

circumstances in your life in which you have to disobey established authority in order to obey God?

3. *Study the following verses on worship and devotion: Exodus 15:11; Deuteronomy 6:5; Psalms 29:2; 45:11; 73:25; Isaiah 26:4; Revelation 19:10; 22:8–9. What are some words that are synonymous with worship? Is it ever appropriate to worship another human being? What is the difference between being appreciative or affirming and worship?*

4. *Your husband needs your counsel in the same ways that you need his. Study these verses on the benefits of godly counsel: Proverbs 12:15; 13:10; 19:20. Are you willing to both receive counsel and to give it? Which is harder for you? Why?*

5. *How would you characterize the dance that you and your husband are dancing? Is it more like Swing, the Twist, Boot Stompin' Boogie, or a Waltz? Why? What would following your husband's lead in your marriage look like? Do you make it easy for him to lead? What does it take for your husband to lead you? Does he have to drag you along, be watchful that you aren't grinding your heel into his foot, or will gentle pressure prompt creative and joyful movement on your part?*

6. *Submission to your husband begins with submission to the Lord. Study James 4:10 and 1 Peter 5:6–7. How do these verses encourage your heart?*

7. *What is your husband's calling? Even if he isn't a believer, what are his gifts? How can you help him exercise these gifts to God's greater glory?*

8. *Summarize what you've learned in this chapter in three or four sentences.*

chapter 10 Created to Communicate

She opens her mouth in wisdom, and the
teaching of kindness is on her tongue.

∽ PROVERBS 31:26

IN THE BEGINNING, THE TRUTH SPOKE

In Genesis, even before the creation of man, God spoke. "'Let there be light,'" He said, "and there was light" (Genesis 1:3). God's first recorded words were ones of creative power and self-revelation. His words formed the light that would place His person and Creation on display to man, and at the end of that day He pronounced that His Creation was "good."

God's first words to mankind were words of blessing, commission, and instruction. He told them of their calling and His provision for them (Genesis 1:28–30). God's words brought benefit to them.

God exhibited man as the pinnacle of His creation by enabling him to speak; because of God's great power, this gift of speech has been passed down to all of Adam and Eve's progeny. Neurobiologists affirm that even before a child is born, the area of his brain that enables speech has begun to develop. Human children continue to be genetically predestined by God to understand and employ words.[1] What's even more interesting and relevant to our topic is that, as every parent knows, *little girls excel at speech.*

WHAT LITTLE GIRLS ARE MADE OF

Lise Eliot reports: "One recent study found that as early as midgestation, female fetuses move their mouths significantly more than male fetuses, as if already practicing for a lifetime of speech. Girl babies start talking a month or two earlier than boys, and their phrases and sentences tend to be longer."[2]

Although these differences tend to even out somewhat as children develop, adult women continue to "do better on tests of verbal fluency and other tasks, like thinking up words that all begin with a particular letter."[3] In general, women are "superior to men in language skills"[4] and enjoy language more than men, as is consistently demonstrated by the overwhelming number of women in linguistics courses in universities.

Along with their dominance in the field of linguistics, women also significantly outnumber men in departments of education, nursing, psychology, and sociology, disciplines that are particularly suited to our helper/nurturer design. Men, on the other hand, excel in math and abstract thought, evidenced by the fact that of the present top one hundred grand masters of chess, only one is female (World Chess Federation rankings, May 2002). Men outnumber women in all math and science courses and in philosophy, geography, history, and engineering (although a woman, Admiral Grace Murray Hopper, developed the first program that translated English language instructions into the language of the target computer). Some may say that these disparities exist because of gender-role stereotypes, but is it logical to assume that, given the emphasis on gender equality in the last thirty years, these discrepancies would continue?

These differences do not occur just because girls are socialized differently from boys. They have been demonstrated by the differences in the "basic structure of men's and women's linguistic brains" and are seen in the differences in development of language skills in male/ female fraternal twins.[5]

This is borne out by the fact that even with twins, girls outdistance boys with their language skills. "Sarah had fraternal twins—a boy and girl—and was astonished by the difference in their language growth. By 18 months her daughter had already gone through the vocabulary growth spurt while her son seemed more interested in vehicles than in language. He had only forty words in his productive vocabulary, and many of them were specific names for the cars in his collection." "The data from the most comprehensive study to date . . . suggest that on average girls lead boys on every language indicator: the number of words produced, the number of words understood, the number of words used in combinations, sentence complexity, and maximum sentence length."[6]

WOMEN ARE PARTICULARLY GIFTED TO HELP

As we've already learned, woman was created by God first to glorify Him, and then to companion her husband and to help him fulfill God's calling on his life. Because of God's purpose in creating us, women were specifically gifted to communicate, to be more aware of social interactions, to be more empathetic and intuitive. (Yet although women seem more intuitive than men, it's important we don't assume that we know what anyone else is thinking or what they're motivations are. It's impossible for us to really understand even our own hearts, let alone the heart of another. Remember, only God knows the heart.)

Aside from obvious anecdotal proof that women excel in these areas, scientific studies also prove this out. For instance, baby girls (even those less than two weeks old), demonstrate greater empathetic awareness because they cry more frequently than baby boys do when they hear other babies cry. They are also more aware and responsive to the emotions of others around them, as evidenced by the fact that they smile earlier than their male counterparts. Even among toddlers, little girls' play is more social and relational (playing house, singing to their "babies," even when they are given only blocks of wood to play with), while little boys tend to strive to rule, create, and order their world (making blocks into "things" such as cars and trains; seeking to dominate others and their surroundings).

Although we live in a culture where such gender-talk is considered archaic, the scientific facts speak clearly: There are intellectual differences between the sexes.[7] I'm not saying that men generally have higher IQs than women, because on the average, there is no disparity between the IQ scores of men and women. I am simply saying that, in general, women excel in certain areas and men in others and that there are patterns and exceptions (for example, men who excel in language and women who excel in math and abstract reasoning) to observe. Indeed, wouldn't it follow that there would be both similarity and dissimilarity between the mental capacities of the sexes, since they were both created to glorify God but have differing roles?

- Have you ever considered the differences between men and women a blessing from God?

- Do you get frustrated when it seems that your husband doesn't think like you or relate the way you do? It's humorous for me to think about the differences in the way that my husband reports on conversations, in comparison to the way I would. I'm interested in nuances and intuitive understanding. I want to know what was "really" being said in the conversation, while he tends to just report facts. Again, I'm not saying that this is true always in every case, just that there are norms of perception differences between the genders.

- Do you value your ability to be empathetic and intuitive? Do you use these gifts to help your husband? Have you ever used this ability to hurt or attack your husband?

- Do you recognize that, as a woman, your language gifting is generally stronger than your husband's? A godly woman will recognize that, just as a husband must control his physical power over his wife, a godly woman must refuse to "abuse" her husband with her more highly developed language, intuition skills, and empathetic understanding of his heart.

THE FIRST LIES

Although man was to use his gift to glorify his Creator by disclosing His nature and will to others, words were soon employed in the attempt to overthrow God's kingdom and impugn His character.

Satan, in the form of the serpent, questioned the veracity of God's words. "Has God said you will die?" he queried. "You surely will not die!" He used God's good gift, speech, to speak blasphemies about Him. Then, Eve abused her gift by misquoting God's command and by influencing her husband to follow her into sin. As you can see, from the very beginning, Satan sought to oust God's rule over our speech since he is, as Jesus calls him, "a liar and the father of lies" (John 8:44). After sinning, Adam used words to try to avert God's holy gaze by blaming Eve for his wickedness. "The woman You gave me," he said as he tried to shift the blame from himself to God for giving him such a helper!

In pronouncing judgment upon Adam, God referred not only to his disobedience in eating the forbidden fruit but first mentioned his sin of listening "to the voice of [his] wife" (Genesis 3:17). Please don't get the wrong idea! It isn't sinful for men to listen to their wives, for in Genesis 21:12, God specifically commands Abraham to listen to Sarah, something he might have been loathe to do after the debacle with Hagar.[8] It isn't sinful for a man to listen to his wife—*unless she is telling him to disobey God.* God provided help for husbands by creating wives who were strong communicators. You know, He could have created wives who were mute like the animals! Instead, He created women who were in His image, able to use speech to communicate. Wise women employ this gift for their husbands' good, and wise men value it.

LET THERE BE LIGHT!

God triumphed over Satan's attempt to usurp speech by sending the Incarnate Word, the Light of the World, Jesus Christ, to proclaim truth and to empower His church to preach the blessed words of life. In the Garden of Gethsemane, Satan tempted Jesus to use words to demand His own way. But our Lord didn't sin with His mouth. Instead, He said, "Not My will, but Yours be done" (Luke 22:42). These words continue to stand as the most blessed example of godly speech ever spoken. They not only set the pattern for all of our talk, they also are the key to our ability to reclaim this gift for God's glory. Christ spoke these words, and because He did so, we who are His are enabled to, as well.

During the Lord's earthly ministry, He communicated the truth to His hearers. With words and in language the people would understand, He taught them, comforted them, rebuked and informed them, and told them of the days to come. Only during the time after His death, before His resurrection, was He silent. Although He wasn't speaking for us to hear during this time, He was in His Father's presence, communicating and fellowshipping with Him. Jesus' "dead body remained on earth and was buried, but His spirit passed immediately into the presence of God in heaven"[9]

It is shocking to consider that the human voice of the Incarnate Word *was silenced for three days* as He paid the penalty for "every careless word" (Matthew 12:36) that we've spoken. The only One who never told a lie, never passed on gossip, told unfit jokes, blasphemed, or questioned God was muted for a time by our sin.

166

- Do you consider speech a precious gift from God?

- Do you consider that your ability to speak is one way that you're like Him? Which father—Your heavenly Father, or Satan, the father of lies—do the patterns of your speech imitate?

- What is the ramification of Jesus' name, "The Incarnate Word"? What does it mean to you?

- If I had a tape recording of your words over the past week, what would I learn about God? Do your words bring light and grace to listeners, especially to your husband?

- Do you consider that Christ died, not only for your sinful actions, but also for your sinful words?

GOD-GLORIFYING WORDS

As with everything else in life, our aim in communication should be to glorify and please the Lord (2 Corinthians 5:9). The startling truth about speech is that our words either serve to glorify and please Him or they exalt and please ourselves. They either portray Him properly, as a highly polished mirror reflects one who gazes into it, or they offer to the world a shattered and tarnished image of His person. Our words will either serve to proclaim the truth about our glorious, loving Father, or they won't; they will either serve to reveal the oneness in the Trinity, or they will distort it. As you can see, one of the primary tools God has given us to reflect His nature and person to the world is our words, and it's to that end we should seek to excel in their use. God has enriched our lives, especially in our role as helpers, by granting us this gift and entreating us to employ it for His glory and our husbands' good.

A DEEP WELL FILLED WITH WORDS

It's easy to think that God-glorifying speech is what we say on Sunday morning during our worship time or when we're having biblical fellowship. And it's true that God is glorified in our praises and when we're praying for or encouraging one another. Godly speech, however, is much more than that. It starts with the way that we view life, with whether we have a godward focus. It's revealed by the words that I speak in my heart when someone cuts me off on the freeway or when I'm drinking lemonade on my back patio, enjoying the spring flowers. Our words are simply the overflow of the thoughts of our hearts, as Jesus said. "The mouth speaks out of that which fills the heart" (Matthew 12:34; *see also* 15:18).

The words that those around me might hear from my lips first had their origin in my heart, in the thoughts that I entertain. When I find myself saying inconsiderate words to my husband, that's more than a trifling rudeness or even sinful disrespect; it's a reflection of my heart and a statement about my view of God's goodness. My words tell all who hear that my heart is filled with self-exaltation and pride, and worse yet, they loudly proclaim that He isn't as good as He says He is. They display a heart that hasn't yet bowed with Jesus in Gethsemane and said, "Not my will, but Yours."

- Generally speaking, what do your words (even when you're not specifically speaking about the Lord) tell others (especially your husband) about God's beauty and the value of knowing Him?

- Think back to the last time you thought, *Why did I say that!?!* What was it you said? Why were you ashamed by your words? Do you see that your words are a reflection of your heart?

"DON'T YOU KNOW WHO I AM?"

Recently, Phil and I were having dinner at a local Mexican restaurant. As the waiters brought us our various courses, we had the opportunity to observe a couple who was seated nearby. Apparently the woman had become unhappy with the presentation of her chicken fajitas and demanded that they be redone for her. Even though the servers tried to accommodate her, she became more and more indignant and insulting as her waiters scurried around. Finally, when her fury reached its zenith she demanded, "Don't you know who I am?" In that moment of her humiliation (which she saw as her exaltation), her heart was graphically revealed, and I felt both embarrassment for her and ashamed of myself. Although I don't think I've ever actually declared those words, I saw that I had often thought them. I knew that unless I attacked this deception, it wouldn't be long before I was saying the same thing.

- Have you ever had thoughts like the one described above? A good way to judge is to assess the words that you use, particularly when dealing with someone who is obligated to give you what you want. How do you treat servers at restaurants? front desk personnel at hotels? checkers at the grocery store?

- Do you see any self-exaltation in your words? Do you ever use phrases such as *"He shouldn't treat me like that!" "I deserve better than this!"* or, *"What a stupid waiter! Why can't he get my order right?"* Do you recognize the disparity between "Not my will, but Yours" and statements like those above?

- Even if you don't actually give voice to phrases like those above, do you ever *think* them?

- Have you ever said anything like that to your husband? What do the words you say to him in anger or frustration reveal about your heart? your view of your calling? God's goodness in giving your husband to you? What do they say about your appraisal of God's wisdom, power, and love?

WORDS AND MEDITATIONS

Psalm 19 is a rich treasure trove filled with gems about God's speech. It declares the ways in which God has created the world so that it speaks of His glory, and it's a perfect example for us to consider as we think about our speech. Psalm 19 begins,

The heavens are telling of the glory of God;
And their expanse is declaring the work of His hands.
Day to day pours forth speech,
And night to night reveals knowledge. . . .
Their line has gone out through all the earth,
And their utterances to the end of the world.
(Psalm 19:1–4)

As these verses show, God continually reveals Himself to man through the Creation. Next, after declaring His glory in Creation, God speaks of the perfections of His Word.

The law of the Lord is perfect, restoring the soul;
The testimony of the Lord is sure, making wise the simple.
The precepts of the Lord are right, rejoicing the heart;
The commandment of the Lord is pure, enlightening the eyes. . . .
The judgments of the Lord are true; they are righteous altogether.
They are more desirable than gold, yes, than much fine gold;
Sweeter also than honey and the drippings of the honeycomb.
Moreover, by them Your servant is warned;
In keeping them there is great reward.
(Psalm 19:7–11).

God's Word is perfect, restores us, is solid, makes us wise. It is right and pure, bringing rejoicing and enlightenment. It is true, righteous, and desirable; it warns and rewards those who heed it. The psalmist continues:

Who can discern his errors? Acquit me of hidden faults.
Also keep back your servant from presumptuous sins;
Let them not rule over me;
Then I will be blameless,
And I shall be acquitted of great transgression.
Let the words of my mouth and the meditation of my heart
Be acceptable in Your sight,
O Lord, my rock and my Redeemer.
(Psalm 19:12–14)

His Word reveals the "thoughts and intentions of the heart" (Hebrews 4:12), exposing our hidden errors and faults. It enables us to throw off the yoke of slavery to sin and shows us the pathway to forgiveness. Since your heart is the source of your words, prayerfully reflect on these questions.

- Do you hear God speaking to you in Creation? What is He saying?
- Do you hear and heed His Word? Do you value it? Meditate on it?
- Do you seek to hide it in your heart through memorization?

The "words of [our] mouth" will only be pleasing to the Lord when the "meditations of [our] heart" are centered on His glory and truth. Remember that learning to count to ten before you speak or learning to make at least one positive statement before you bring correction will only be *self-serving manipulations* if your heart isn't focused on reflecting and pleasing Him.

You might be wondering why I'm spending so much time discussing God's Word when what we're interested in is our words, especially those we speak to our husbands. I've concentrated on this simply because *God's speech sets the pattern that we are to follow.* His Word uniquely brings us light and changes our hearts. Our words, particularly those to our husbands, should mirror His Word by bringing light, encouragement, truth, joy, warning, and correction.

- Do you regularly declare the work of His hands? Do you help your husband understand God's gracious activity in your lives?

- Do you humbly seek to reveal your heart to your husband? Do you confess your sin specifically and frequently? Do you ask for forgiveness and declare your imperfections?[10]

- Do you warn your husband when he is erring? Do you speak about the reward of God-centered obedience?

- Do you seek to restore or turn your husband toward obedient trust? In Hebrew, *shub* is the word translated "restore," which means "to return or go back." Are your words those of a wise woman, instructing and enlightening your husband?

- Are your words pure and delightful? Do they bring rejoicing and comfort to his heart?

- Do you help your husband discern his errors? As his wife, you are in a unique position to show him, as a mirror does, areas of his heart that might be hidden from his view. Do you seek to cover his sin by striving to turn him back from error (James 5:20)?

- Do you encourage him with your godly words? Do you speak to him about the joys of meditating on the Lord and His Word?

A WOMAN'S WORDS

Like most women, I love to communicate. In fact, I love it so much

I do it for a living. I particularly enjoy articulating my opinion and perspectives. I love sharing my heart with words that succinctly display the depths of my despair and the heights of my joy. Communication is a wonderful gift, isn't it? But as a woman, I also face grave temptations to use this gift in a wicked way.

The Bible speaks specifically to both men and women about their words and, as we've already seen in the case of Adam and Eve, gives plenty of examples of sinful speech by both. It is interesting, however, that women are particularly instructed to control their speech in one specific area: gossip. Women prove their fitness for leadership by avoiding gossip (1 Timothy 3:11), while in the same passage, men are exhorted not to lie or be "double-tongued" (v. 8). It is interesting that although there are several non-gender-specific injunctions against gossip or talebearing in the Bible, men are not specifically warned against it the way that women are (see 1 Timothy 3:11; 5:13; Titus 2:3). Men are exhorted about their speech, but those exhortations are more along the lines of lying, proud boasting, and angry words.

Women most frequently sin with their words in relational ways, reflecting their created design. *Remember, gossip and talebearing always involve relationships.* Men most frequently sin with their words in connection with their calling to rule (lying, bragging, harsh words). So, as a woman, you'll need to guard against sinful speech, particularly in the area of your relationships.

- How much time do you spend on the phone? How much *profitable* time do you spend on the phone? In light of Proverbs 10:19, how much time *should* you spend on the phone?

Women are also warned about nagging and contentious words: "The contentions of a wife are a constant dripping" (Proverbs 19:13; see also Proverbs 21:9, 19; 25:24; 27:15–16). A wife who doesn't control her language has the power to make her husband miserable.

A WIFE'S WORDS

As we come to the close of this chapter, let's think specifically about how a wife can help her husband through her use of words.

SPEAK TO GOD FIRST

A wife should first and primarily speak to God in prayer. Time spent each day in heart-humbling prayer will do more to transform your speech than anything else. Plead with God to purify the meditations of your heart so that the words that flow from it will be pure as well.

PLEASANT, HEALTHFUL WORDS

Second, a wife should use words that are pleasant and flow with sweetness, as Proverbs 16:24 says: "Pleasant words are a honeycomb, sweet to the soul and healing to the bones." Do you express gratitude and thankfulness to your husband? Do you point out evidences of grace in his life? Jay Adams comments on Proverbs 16:24:

> The present verse has nothing to do with flattery; it is speaking of helpful speech that meets the needs of others. The words are *pleasant* and flow with *sweetness to the soul* and *healing to the bones* of those undergoing affliction and trouble. Here is the picture of a truly biblical counselor [and godly wife] who wields God's Word well in the blessing of others.[11]

GRACEFUL, DELIBERATE WORDS

Colossians 4:6 says, "Let your speech always be with grace, as though seasoned with salt, so that you will know how you should respond to each person." How do you respond to your husband? Do you respond with words that give strength, faith, and grace? How do you respond when he disappoints you or crosses your will?

TRUTHFUL YET LOVING WORDS

Ephesians 4:15 says, "But speaking the truth in love, we are to grow up in all aspects into Him who is the head, even Christ." It's easy for me to fall into one of two errors: I either avoid speaking the truth (because I'm fearful or apathetic), or I speak it in an unloving manner. A wise woman learns how to combine both facets of godly speech: truth and love into communication that brings both light and delight to her husband.

WISE, KIND, AND COMFORTING WORDS

The virtuous woman in Proverbs 31 teaches those around her with wisdom and kindness, similar to the truthful, yet loving, speech referred to above. When Job was in the middle of great distress he cried, "For the despairing man there should be kindness from his friend; so that he does not forsake the fear of the Almighty. My brothers have acted deceitfully like a wadi" (Job 6:14–15). Job's counselors were as "undependable as intermittent streams." He says that they dashed his hope in the same way that weary travelers who turned aside from their normal route in the hope of finding water, only to discover a dry creek bed, had their hopes crushed. How often has your husband been distressed or disappointed because you've proven to be a dry mirage instead of a cool, refreshing spring?

God has uniquely crafted wives to be our husband's helper and companion—and it's by His design and power that you'll be able to grow in this calling. If you're like me, you desire to become a fountain of refreshing, wise, and kind words. As you consider the questions that follow, remind yourself of the joyful truth that the Word was made flesh, in part so that your speech would reflect the blessed speech of Your Father.[12]

Finding and Fulfilling Your Calling

1. *Read James 3:2–12. What are the word pictures James paints of the tongue? What are the incongruities he points out? How powerful is speech?*

2. *Would your husband say, with Solomon, "Your lips, my bride, drip honey; Honey and milk are under your tongue" (Song of Songs 4:11). Why did you answer the way you did?*

3. *Read the following verses on speech: Proverbs 10:20–21; 12:18; 14:3; 15:23; 16:23; 18:6–7; 20:15. What does Proverbs teach us about speech?*

4. *The apostle Paul was comforted by Titus' report (2 Corinthians 7:6–7). Do you consistently seek to comfort your husband, especially when he's down or troubled?*

5. *Are you accustomed to speaking about your own struggles and sins? Do you know how to ask for forgiveness specifically, rather than just saying, "Sorry"?*

6. *Summarize the teaching of this chapter in four or five sentences.*

chapter 11   # Helping Your Husband Believe

" . . . just as Sarah obeyed Abraham, calling him lord . . . you have become her children if you do what is right without being frightened by any fear."

∞1 PETER 3:6

When the Lord looked at Adam, unmarried and alone, He declared that his situation wasn't good. So, in response to Adam's need, God created Eve: a woman, taken from his side, consisting of his own flesh, in many ways completing him. Eve was to be Adam's companion, helper, and co-regent over the world God had created for them. Together they knew intimate fellowship, oneness in purpose, great love, and mutual respect as they fulfilled God's call on their individual lives.

In God's providence, however, sin entered that holy union, and Adam and Eve (and all their descendants) were thrust into a world permeated with confusion, disobedience, unbelief, and misery. Our present condition is that even the most blessed, godly marriages are filled with the consequences of sin: disobedience, unbelief, and misery. No couple has completely escaped the ravages of that reality, and even those who come the closest to doing so are ultimately torn apart in death. Paradise, as the first married couple knew it, has been lost, and we won't truly experience it again until we eat from the "tree of life which is in the Paradise of God" (Revelation 2:7). In that glorious day, we'll experience an unhindered understanding of each other, and we'll behold the glorious realities of the Trinity, of unity perfectly blended with diversity . . . a vision that will bring us great joy and delight. But, in the meantime, we're all stuck in the "not yet" of today and we need to know how to please and glorify God in this life.

COMMON TEMPTATIONS AND LOGS IN OUR EYES

In the chapters that precede this one, I've purposely focused on a woman and wife's calling before God and her husband. I've sought to construct a foundation for you to think about yourself as a woman, created in the image of God, called to glorify Him. I sought to help you see yourself as a wife, created to companion and help your husband. In all of this, I've been very purposeful in focusing on your calling and avoided talking about your husband's foibles. I've done that for two reasons.

The first is that God calls us to fulfill our calling in the very circumstances that we're in. The only opportunity you have to fulfill your calling and obey the Lord is in the now. You can't fulfill God's call in the past or in the future—you've only got today, this minute— to choose to follow Him or to turn aside.

One of the ways that my sinful heart frequently deceives me is by tricking me into thinking that, if only my circumstances were different, if it were just yesterday or tomorrow, I would be obedient. If only I had a different husband, child, vocation, church, or home, I would perfectly fulfill God's call. The pity of this is that it works so often in my life! Yes, I persistently think, *If Phil were just . . . and my kids were just . . . and my church was just . . . then I would be truly holy!* The truth that the Holy Spirit speaks into this deception is that God has called us to obey Him with the husband we now have; so in one sense, it doesn't really matter what he's like.

Now, in saying this, I don't mean that our husbands' sin or unbelief doesn't ultimately matter to the Lord or to the building of His kingdom, or that it doesn't break our hearts. What I mean is that our obedience is not contingent upon their spirituality, although I commonly act as though it is. I also don't mean to sound hard-nosed and say, "Tough luck; just obey." The truth is, though, that the only hope there is (aside from being transported to an alternate reality) is to learn to see God approaching you in love and for your good in the difficulty you're presently facing.

When I start the "If Phil were" process, I think the enemy of my soul has been identified and is sleeping by my side. No, *this enemy* is closer than that: *this enemy resides in my heart.* As I grouse about my circumstances and how, if they were just changed, I would be able to obey the Lord, I'm deceived and I'm forgetting the precious promise in 1 Corinthians 10:13. Let me remind you again that

> *no temptation has overtaken you but such as is common to man; and God is faithful, who will not allow you to be tempted beyond what you are able, but with the temptation will provide the way of escape also, so that you will be able to endure it.* (1 Corinthians 10:13)

God's Word is clear: He has promised to be with us in every temptation and to guard us from any situation wherein obedience would be impossible; we are to rule over our sin in every circumstance.

- Do you believe that obedience is always possible, even in the circumstances you face?

- Do you believe that God rules sovereignly in your life and uses even your sins and mistakes for His glory and your good?

- The "way of escape" Paul spoke of didn't refer to fleeing from your trial, except perhaps in the realization that heaven will ultimately be yours. It meant that God will help you find the way out of the misery and defeat of it. Is there any specific area of misery you experience in your marriage? How would faithful performance of your calling change your circumstance or your view of it? How has your trial been complicated by your sinful response to it?

HERE, DEAR, LET ME GET THAT SPECK OUT OF YOUR EYE

I've also avoided talking about our husband's failures because most of us are already pretty good at assessing them. After all, we're intuitively tuned in to our spouses—right? If you're like me, it's pretty easy to focus on how your husband is failing, while ignoring your own gross inconsistencies and sin. So, I've spent ten chapters challenging you to take in and take up God's call on your life. That's not because I'm averse to looking at the sin in my husband's life; it's just that I want to be sure that I've followed Matthew 7:3–5 before doing so.

Why do you look at the speck that is in your [husband's] eye, but do not notice the log that is in your own eye? Or how can you say to your [husband], "Let me take the speck out of your eye," and behold, the log is in your own eye? You hypocrite, first take the log out of your own eye, and then you will see clearly to take the speck out of your [husband's] eye. (Matthew 7:3–5 paraphrased)

You know, Jesus could have said, "Don't look at the speck in your husband's eye!" couldn't He? Instead, He gave us how-to directions. It's loving and fitting for me to think deeply about the sin and unbelief in my husband, but before I do so, I must think even more deeply about my own sin and unbelief. I must spend serious time looking in the mirror of His Word and, with the magnifying glass of the Holy Spirit, examine my heart. So, before we think about how to help our husbands in their disobedience or unbelief, I have to ask you: Are you a believer? I don't mean "Do you believe in Jesus?" because I doubt that you would have spent this much time reading this book if you didn't. What I mean is:

- Do you believe that God rules lovingly, sovereignly, wisely, and powerfully in your life?

- Do you believe that Jesus Christ died to save sinners, and that the only recommendation you bring to Him is your sin?

- Do you believe that the Holy Spirit's power is effective to save even the vilest of sinners?

- Do you see that, although you're saved, you're not perfectly holy and that the "law of sin" still works mightily in you, so that the good you want, you don't do, but you practice the very evil that you do not want to practice (see Romans 7:19–23)? What sins do you recognize in your own heart? Have you repented of them, and are you trusting in grace to remove them? Have you confessed your habitual sins to your husband and asked for his prayerful help?

- Do you believe that Jesus Christ patiently bears with all your sin and prays for you daily, even though you've spurned Him many times?

- Do you trust that there will come one glorious day when you're freed from all your sin and bondage; that on that day (and only on that day), you'll be able to see your sin and your Savior as they really are; and that, in the meantime, your heavenly Father has committed Himself to beautify and purify you for His glory?

If you believe these things, you're ready to help your husband with his unbelief and sin. If you can't answer in the affirmative, then stop now and bow in humble prayer before Him. You might pray something like this:

Heavenly Father,
I thank You that You've so lovingly called me to Yourself. You
did that when I was filthy and rebellious. Even though You've
now granted me the perfections of Your Son and declared me
righteous in Your sight, I still spurn Your attentions more
times than I even know by . . . (add your own words here).
Father, please make my heart tender and sensitive to my own
sins. Help me to be more aware and troubled by them (name
them), than I am by my husband's sin. Give me the grace to
lovingly cover his sin when it's right to do so, and help me to
help him by lovingly, gently, and patiently confronting him
when it would displease You to do otherwise. Help me to be
wise enough to know the difference. Help me to remember
Your patience when dealing with me and cause me to treat my
husband the way I would want to be treated. Help me to
believe that You are lovingly overruling every detail in my life
and that one day, I'll see You as You are, and I'll hear You
say, "Enter into the joy of your Lord, dearest bride!"

DISOBEDIENT HUSBANDS AND BEAUTIFUL WIVES

We're going to spend the remainder of this chapter reviewing
one of the most succinct passages in the New Testament on this
topic. The passage is found in 1 Peter 3:1–6. Even if you're already
familiar with this portion of Scripture, please take time to read it
over.

In the same way, you wives, be submissive to your own husbands so
that even if any of them are disobedient to the word, they may be won
without a word by the behavior of their wives, as they observe your
chaste and respectful behavior. Your adornment must not be merely
external—braiding the hair, and wearing gold jewelry, or putting on
dresses; but let it be the hidden person of the heart, with the imperish-
able quality of a gentle and quiet spirit, which is precious in the sight

of God. For in this way in former times the holy women also, who hoped in God, used to adorn themselves, being submissive to their own husbands; just as Sarah obeyed Abraham, calling him lord, and you have become her children if you do what is right without being frightened by any fear.

When Peter penned these words, he was writing to a church under siege. The beginning of his letter identifies his readers as those who had been scattered, who were being "distressed by various trials" (1 Peter 1:6), whose faith was being tried in a furnace (4:12–13).

In penning this letter, Peter was acting as a loving shepherd, encouraging his flock and warning them about the temptations that they would face in persecution. He sought to embolden them as they braved great tribulation and cautioned them not to give up or give in to sin because the battle was waging hot. In doing so, he spoke specifically to citizens living under ungodly rulers, servants with unjust masters, and wives with disobedient husbands.

IN THE SAME WAY

Peter begins his encouraging treatise to wives who were suffering persecution in their own home by reminding them of the example of their Lord and the ultimate purpose in their suffering. "In the same way" (1 Peter 3:1), he wrote,

You have been called for this purpose, since Christ also suffered for you, leaving you an example for you to follow in His steps, who committed no sin, nor was any deceit found in His mouth; and while being reviled, He did not revile in return; while suffering, He uttered no threats, but kept entrusting Himself to Him who judges righteously; and He Himself bore our sins in His body on the cross, so that we might die to sin and live to righteousness. (1 Peter 2:21–24)

Peter's point is clear: The key for Christians, in general, and wives, in particular, to persevere through hard times is by fixing their attention and trust on the One who has gone before them: Jesus Christ. (See also 1 Peter 1:7; 3:9, 18; 4:1, 13.) It's astonishing that the Son of God should suffer so at the hands of ungodly men, but that example, as great as it is, isn't enough. If He hadn't also brought us new life, we wouldn't be able to "die to sin and live to righteousness." You see, He's set the example *and* He's given us the power to follow Him. So, I can say to you today, in the middle of the fierce persecution in your own home, *Look to Jesus! Trust Him, follow Him, lean wholly on Him! He's marked out the way and He'll be there for you now.*

- Is your heart focused on the Lord and His sacrifice and empowering love rather than on your husband's ungodly actions?

- Would you say that in this trial you "greatly rejoice with joy inexpressible and full of glory" because "though you have not seen Him, you love Him, and though you do not see Him now, [you] believe in Him" (1 Peter 1:8)?

- Is your faith contingent upon seeing change in your husband? Do you become sinfully angry when he continues in sin? Are you sinfully elated when he does what you think he should do? In asking these questions, I'm not saying that it's wrong to grieve over sin or rejoice when righteousness prevails. What I am saying is that the foundation of your grief and joy should be God's glory and His loving providence, not your husband's day-to-day responses. So the question remains: Is your faith resting on anything other than the Lord's faithfulness?

SUBMISSION TO GOD'S AUTHORITY

As we saw in chapter 9, our submission as wives is actually rooted in our submission to Christ and the Father's established authority. It's very tempting to think that my submission to my husband will occur when and if he gets his act together. After all, *Why should I be obedient and submit when he's not doing what I think he should be doing?* But Peter counters that thought throughout his letter. (For instance, see 1 Peter 2:12, 13, 15, 18–20.)

How does Peter encourage those who were suffering under ungodly authority? After reminding them of Christ's example and power, He tells them to excel in obedience and submission! He continually directs them to look at the big picture: Their obedience is pleasing to God . . . it silences foolish men . . . it serves as a witness to the lost.

- Do you keep the "big picture" in mind when you struggle with submission?
- Do you recognize that the suffering of the godly pleases God (1 Peter 2:19; 3:14–17)? Does that really matter?
- Do you see your obedience as one of the means God may use to turn your husband's heart?

It's obvious that Peter wanted Christians to be known by their humility, obedience, and desire to please the Lord, but that didn't mean he wanted them to silently acquiesce to ungodliness. Rather, in the midst of their ungodly situation, they were to "proclaim the excellencies of Him who [has] called [them] out of darkness into His marvelous light" (1 Peter 2:9). They were to continue to speak of His grace and their new life, even though they were surrounded by unbelievers.

Even though Isaiah 53:7 says that Jesus was "silent before [His] shearers" and "did not open His mouth," He did speak to those who were trying Him. He spoke to them the truth about Himself and their authority. He did not lie to them, revile them, or utter any threats, as Peter points out. A wife's response to ungodliness should be patterned after Christ's. She may speak the truth but not in a sinfully self-protective, angry, deceptive, or threatening way.

In 1 Peter 3, Peter gave instruction to wives who were turning to Christ and who needed guidance. Was it proper for them to believe something that their husband disbelieved? Was it fitting for them to follow a different path, to turn to the true God? Should they refuse to worship their husband's idols? What should they do if their husband refused to listen to or obey the preached word? In their circumstance, Peter encouraged them: "Even if any of them are disobedient to the word, they may be won without a word by the behavior of their wives" (v. 1). Christian wives were to affirm their allegiance to the Lord, even if that meant disagreeing with or disobeying their husbands. Peter didn't tell them to follow their husbands in their sin and unbelief, but rather to seek to win them over to their way of thinking.

A PROMISE OF HOPE

Peter sought to encourage wives with hard-hearted husbands that there was hope. His encouragement may be paraphrased in this way:

> If your husband has refused to listen and respond to the preaching of the gospel, there's still hope! He can still be won, even though he won't listen to preaching! Your lifestyle (including your speech) preaches powerfully, and God may use you, instead of a pastor or missionary, as the means to turn him around! Don't despair!

I've frequently heard this passage used as a command to silence, especially when coupled with the mention in verse 4 of a "quiet spirit." Rather than seeing this verse as a command to silence, wives of unbelievers should see it as *a promise of hope*. It is a promise to Christian wives that, when an unbelieving husband has been exposed to the preaching of the gospel and continues to disobey it, God has another means by which He can turn the husband's heart around:

the submissive conduct and respectful, calm, inner beauty of his wife.

> Peter's point is not to prohibit a wife's speaking to her husband about the gospel once he's expressed a lack of interest in it or opposition to it. His point is that she has another resource at her disposal, which God may use instead of spoken witness to break through her husband's hardness of heart. The real issue is not whether or not she ever speaks about her faith to him, but the attitude in which she does it—in fact, in general, whether he sees in her the inner beauty of a gentle or quiet spirit.[1]

Nor does the mention of a "quiet spirit" prohibit respectfully confronting sin in a believing husband's life, since the specific context of this passage *and* all of 1 Peter is how to live a godly life when suffering persecution by unbelievers. Those who wrongfully teach that this verse means that women should not counsel, confront, admonish, encourage, or otherwise *nouthetically* minister to their husbands have legalistically gone beyond Scripture and deprived husbands of one of the greatest means of sanctification: the helper given to them by God.

Christian wives of unbelieving husbands can have great hope that there are other means of communicating the gospel aside from formal preaching! In the context of 1 Peter and especially this passage, wives of unbelieving or disobedient husbands can know a peaceful confidence. (See also 1 Peter 3:15–16.)

THE CONVICTING POWER OF TRUE HOLINESS

How will this message be preached to our husbands? Not by incessant nagging or anxious pestering, nor by schemingly using beautiful clothes and hairstyles. It will be broadcast to them through the megaphone of our heart's attitude, an attitude that's marked by calm assurance and trust.

Peter recognized that a suffering wife may be tempted to use her natural strengths to manipulate her husband. She might use her communication skills to carp at him while she seeks to talk him into the kingdom (or into a more godly lifestyle). She might use his God-given attraction to her beauty to exploit his interest in her or to punish him when he doesn't comply. These manipulations are the marks of a fearful woman—a woman who isn't doing "what is right" (1 Peter 3:6). For the woman whose husband is either an unbeliever or who is habitually disobedient to the Word, warfare must be ceaselessly waged against this fear.

FIGHTING FEAR WITH FAITH AND TRUTH

As you consider your husband's disobedience or unbelief, what are your fears? What are the lies that you have embraced?

- Do you believe that he'll never change? Since God was able to change you, and millions of others like you, why wouldn't He be able to change your husband (Ephesians 2:1–8)?

- Do you think that your children won't serve God unless their father is an obedient believer? The fact that a father disbelieves doesn't guarantee that his children will follow him. The lies of behaviorism are trumped by the lives of Hezekiah and Josiah in the Old Testament and Timothy in the New Testament. Both Hezekiah and Josiah were godly kings who were raised by very wicked fathers (see 2 Chronicles 28–32 [Ahaz and Hezekiah)] and 2 Chronicles 33:21–35:27 for the story of Amon and Josiah). Timothy was raised by an unbelieving Greek father who had refused to allow him to be circumcised (Acts 16:1–3), and yet he came to faith, was used greatly by the Lord, and was mentored by the apostle Paul.

I'm not saying that a godly example is of no value. God may use your husband's godly example as the means to bring your children to faith. On the other hand, He may use your godly response to your husband's unbelief to draw your children toward Him. God sovereignly arranges families according to His predetermined will, and our whole trust is to reside in His goodness and mercy, not on our ability to live lives that will turn our children's dead hearts toward Him. Of course, it is right to train our children in the "nurture and admonition of the Lord," but only in faithful obedience, not as a method to control any desired outcome. *Only the Holy Spirit makes our children into believers.*

- Do you think that you'll never know true joy unless your husband changes? You're believing the lie that your joy and peace are contingent upon your husband's obedience. You're forgetting that Jesus Christ has promised you *both* tribulation *and* peace in this world (John 16:33) and that your hope is in Him because He has "overcome the world."

- Do you believe that in marrying your husband you made a mistake that God can't redeem? Perhaps you sinfully married an unbeliever or someone that your parents or pastor counseled you against marrying. Although we do suffer temporal consequences for our sins, the eternal consequences have been eradicated in Christ. Not only will you not have to pay a penalty for disobedience, but now even your disobedience can become a blessing in your life as you learn to hate sin and love righteousness. God uses everything in our life, even our sin, to draw us to Himself and to teach us to long for Him alone. God is more powerful than you can possibly imagine, and if you are His, He loves you with a love that overcomes all obstacles and turns darkness into light.

PRECIOUS ATTITUDES

Peter encourages wives that rather than relying on outward strength or beauty, we should develop hearts that are chaste, respectful, gentle, quiet, and obedient. These hearts may be the means that He will use to draw your husband to Himself. But even if you don't see any great changes in your husband, you can rest in the truth that God is being glorified and you're becoming more and more like the Lord Jesus every day.

HOPELESS AND HELPLESS

Betty wept as she spoke to me about her sin and discouragement in her marriage. "I know that I shouldn't have married Bill," she said, "but I thought he was a Christian. Now he won't attend church with the kids, and I'm afraid that they won't serve the Lord either. I've tried praying for him in special ways and leaving tracts around the house. I've even read the Bible to him in his sleep. I try to wear the clothes he likes, even though they're risqué, and I've even watched sexually explicit videos with him so he'll listen to me, but nothing works. I get so tired of trying over and over to please him without seeing any results that sometimes I just scream at him. What should I do?"

How would you answer Betty? Is she focused on the inner qualities that are precious in the sight of God? Is she seeking to develop a heart that's chaste, respectful, gentle, quiet, and obedient? She is rightfully concerned with her husband's salvation, but the means she's employing reveal a heart that's full of fear and desperation. What would you say to her about her beliefs and the behavior that flows from them?

- Is her behavior "chaste"? Is it modest and pure? Has she put off the ungodly emphasis on outer beauty, seeking to please the Lord instead of acquiescing to her husband's sinful demands? Has she sought to beautify her inner self by meditating on God's faithfulness and sustaining power? Is she trusting in God or in herself? There's nothing wrong with beautifying yourself in ways that please your husband. Beauty isn't sinful; only trust in it as a means of manipulating your husband is.

- Is her behavior "respectful"? Does she demonstrate a godly reverence and fear of the Lord and the authority He has placed in her life? Does she fear the Lord more than her husband's displeasure? Is she willing to respectfully stand against his sin?

- Is she gentle or mild? Does she recognize that God is powerful enough to turn even her husband's heart so that she doesn't have to be demanding or force him into faith?

- Is she quiet? This word *quiet* doesn't mean that she is silent. Instead it refers to an inner attitude of peaceful—not fearful or resentful—calm.

PRECIOUS WOMEN

Near my house there is a small lake. On some windless mornings when I drive over it, the water glassily reflects the foothills that surround it. I love to gaze at it and consider what this calmness teaches me. *Is my heart like that lake?* I wonder. *Is it calm, peacefully reflecting the truths of God's faithfulness and great love?* Sometimes it is. At other times, though, my heart is like the ocean during a storm—gray and churning, tossed and agitated—dangerous to be around.

Peter teaches that a gentle and quiet spirit is "precious in the sight of God." His gaze penetrates through all my outward appearances and hypocrisies, and He considers my heart. Is there faith there? Is there trust in His goodness, wisdom, power, and love? Am I calmly resting in Him or wildly kicking against His providence and trying to exert all my power to rearrange my husband's heart? In God's sight, a trusting heart is *precious,* a word that means "of the highest value" or "extremely expensive." What makes this attitude so valuable? First, its rarity, and second, the price that was paid to obtain it. Only a heart that's been drenched in the precious blood of Christ finds its peace and rest in Him. You can rest in Him, lovingly speaking and living truth before your husband, knowing that God holds you gently in the palm of His hand. Your faith is precious to Him and He'll sustain you as you grow in peaceful trust.

Finding and Fulfilling Your Calling

1. *Are you surprised by the fiery trial you're facing? Why? What assumptions have you made about what your life should look like? Do you rejoice in the truth that when you're suffering persecutions you're sharing in them with Christ? Read 1 Peter 4:12–13.*

2. *Read Galatians 6:1–3 and Proverbs 27:5. What do these passages tell us about our obligation to help fellow believers who are entrapped in sin? Why is "open rebuke" better than secret love?*

3. *Isaiah 26:3 reads, "The steadfast of mind You will keep in perfect peace, because he trusts in You." What would steadfastness of mind look like in your life? How is this attitude attained? (See also 1 Chronicles 5:20; 2 Chronicles 16:8–9; 32:8; Psalm 125:1–2.) It is right for you to pray for your husband's salvation and sanctification; but first, why not pray that God would help you grow in trust and reliance upon Him?*

4. *How have you used words in a godly way to help your husband believe and obey? How have you used them in an ungodly way? It's obvious that no one was ever badgered into the kingdom, but we still try, don't we? What will you do instead?*

5. *You are obligated to submit to your unbelieving husband in everything except areas of faith and conscience. In these areas, your husband has no authority. He does not have the authority to command you to sin, since your highest allegiance is to God. Have you compromised your conscience to try to please him? In what way? It might be appropriate for you to plan now what words you'll use the next time this situation arises: how will you respectfully and gently confront him, while at the same time assuring him of your willingness to obey in other matters.*

6. *Summarize this chapter in three or four sentences.*

chapter 12 Women Who Hope in God

Therefore, prepare your minds for action; be self-controlled; set your hope fully on the grace to be given you when Jesus Christ is revealed.

∽ 1 PETER 1:13 NIV

Recently, Phil and I had the joy of taking the eldest of our grandsons, Wesley, to Disneyland. Although the trip from our home takes less than two hours, Wesley was overflowing with anticipation and childlike impatience. "Are we there yet, Mimi?" he wondered over and over. "No, my dearest, not yet—but soon," I replied. "Can we see it yet?" he asked. "Not quite," I said, "but if you close your eyes, we'll be there before you know it." Soon Wesley took the jacket I had placed over his legs and draped it over his head so he could sleep. He reached out from under his "blanket" and held my hand. And then, even though he was sound asleep, it didn't take much to awaken him when we arrived at the Magic Kingdom; just a gentle nudge and a "We're here, my darling" and his eyes flew open and he was ready for fun!

I delight in expressions of childlike joy and anticipation, don't you? One of the most pleasing gifts God has given Phil and me during these last years is the opportunity to experience those qualities again, firsthand. There's just nothing like running across a parking lot, with a toddler in tow, to get to the ticket booth so the fun can begin. We spent many years (almost twenty!) with teenagers in our home, and although they were a delight, I did long for that innocent cherubic expectancy that's one of the hallmarks of a toddler. *Where did that joy go?* I've wondered. *Will I ever see it again?*

CHILDLIKE JOY OR BENIGN RESIGNATION

I've often wondered what happens to joy—is there a happiness hormone that dissipates as we age? Have we lived so long and experienced so much of this sin-cursed world that we've lost the capacity for joy? Where did the hopeful anticipation of our youth go? What happened to the joy in our marriages?

Could it be that, after so many years of conflict and unfulfilled expectations, many women settle down into what my friend Carol Cornish calls "benign resignation"? It's not that we don't try to do what's right or fail to believe that somehow God is using our marriage for His glory; it's just that there are rooms in our hearts that have grown cold and dark. These are places in our relationship with our husband (and our faith in God) that we just don't visit anymore. These cellars of our faith are like relatives we avoid because they always bring us heartache—even though we love them and would really like to see them. We avoid certain topics, not that we agree with our husband or are happy with what's happening, but because we've tried and failed so many times that we've decided that the best strategy is to just close the door and place a Do Not Disturb sign on the knob. This is a malignant truce, a benign resignation.

You might be thinking, *Well, if I'm not sinning outright and if I'm trying to serve my husband in other areas, what's the problem with ignoring these places of conflict and disappointment?* What's the problem? The problem is that *Jesus Christ wants to redeem every area of your life.* When we "play like" or give in to benign resignation, it's a sure sign of residual unbelief, self-protection, and lack of love.

Fine, if that's the way it has to be, we say, *we'll live together for the Lord's sake, but you live your life and I'll live mine! We'll call it a truce. I won't expect anything from you and don't you expect anything from me, and we'll get along just dandy.* Life is never dandy when we ignore a cavernous sinkhole expanding in our relationships. Don't be fooled; this benign resignation isn't dying to yourself or faithful living. It's deception, it's a sham. And we'll never really live until we die to ourselves.

Jesus Christ desires to make you whole and holy, and that means you'll have to expose even your deepest disappointments to His healing hand. I know that it's difficult to look at these areas where we hurt the most and say, "OK, Lord, redeem even this." But it's the only way to holiness. Of course, the truth is that we can only ignore areas of disappointment and conflict for just so long. Soon their presence is felt as they come boiling up from the recesses of our hearts in foul bubbles of angry words, sniping gossip, vile lusts, and indifferent chilliness to our spouse and the Lord.

- Are you aware of any areas of "benign resignation" in your heart?

- Are there any topics you avoid with your husband because you think that there is no hope of reconciliation or resolution? Where have you called a poisonous truce?

- Are there any areas of "darkness" in your relationship with your husband? You'll be able to recognize one by the way you feel when you think about it—afraid, disappointed, or bitterly passive.

- Have you settled into a life of faithless mundanity when it comes to your marriage?

- What would bowing in humble adoration before the Lord look like in this particular circumstance?

- How's your joy quotient? Do you believe that God can bring *real* good out of this?

SILENCING THE SIRENS OF UNBELIEF, SELF-PROTECTION, AND LACK OF LOVE

When I think about the unbelief, self-protection, and lack of love residing in my heart, it's pretty overwhelming. *How will I ever change?* I wonder. The pathway to lasting change isn't through some personal reformation, therapeutic regimen, or even heartfelt resolution to do better. It doesn't even come about by my reading a good book about marriage! No, there's only one path that leads to victory in this arena. It's a path that leads straight into a garden of anguish, an executioner's hill, a cold tomb, and finally, to a glorious new day. The only way to silence your enemies is to die, so that when they call to you, you won't hear them. The siren's song has no effect on the ears of the dead.

Let me help you identify some of the expectations or desires that may have given rise to your disappointments, discouragements, and benign resignations.

- What expectations did you have of your husband? What did you think he would do that he's failed in doing? For instance, did you imagine that he would be a great spiritual leader? Did you suppose that he would rescue you from all your trouble? Did you think that he would always be romantic and attentive?
- What topics are off-limits or taboo with him?
- What have you always wanted to hear him say that he's never said? Sometimes what our hearts crave is dangerously close to worship. We want our husbands to fall at our feet and proclaim that we are the center of their universe; of course, you know that if they did that they would be sinfully idolatrous.

- What have you always wanted to say but were afraid to? What do you need to say?
- What are you afraid of? What do you think you need from your husband in order to be happy?
- What would a joy-filled relationship with the Lord or with your spouse look like?

Our expectations, longings, and desires frequently function as ruling motivations or false gods in our lives. We have false gods when we believe that we must have a certain "something" (other than God) without which we'll never find joy. Because of these strong desires (what the New Testament frequently calls *lusts*), we sin both inwardly and outwardly. We sin outwardly with words and actions that fail to glorify God as we portray the uppermost loves in our hearts. Reigning love for ourselves, our comforts, and our dreams captivates and motivates us. We sin inwardly in our apathetic, passionless faith, and by spinning self-protective cocoons that bind us and blind us. Snares and traps teem in the dark land where our dreams and desires rule.

What hope is there for us but to flee to the Cross? Lay before His bleeding feet your dearest expectations (even those that seem godly), your fondest dreams, your greatest loves. Say to Him,

These are Yours, dearest Lord. My desire to have a husband who does not do [such and such a thing that dismays me] is now and fully Yours. I sacrifice it to Your blood. I thank You that you withheld this from me so that I would trust more wholly in You. Lord, please don't grant this desire if to do so would cause shallowness or sinful elation in my heart. Teach me to trust in You alone. May I learn to embrace Your desires and say with my Lord, "It's not my will that I desire, but Yours alone."

Plead with your Savior to put to death the deceitful charms and expectations that have so cunningly called you and entrapped you in their death grip and strive, by His power, to affirm the good in His plan.

EMBRACE HIS SOVEREIGN WILL

The unbelief that invades our hearts must be assaulted by truth. God rules sovereignly and has lovingly and expressly placed each one of us in the marriage we're in so that we would grow to reflect Him as we were created to. Embrace fully and joyfully His wonderful plan for you. Ponder these verses:

- "I know that You can do all things, and that no purpose of Yours can be thwarted" (Job 42:2). What is God's purpose in placing you in the marriage you're in? Have you tried to thwart God's purpose in your marriage?

- "The steps of a man are established by the Lord, and He delights in his way" (Psalm 37:23). Knowing that God is loving, wise, and good, how would the disappointments you've encountered in your marriage bring delight to God?

- "Many plans are in a man's heart, but the counsel of the Lord will stand" (Proverbs 19:21). How have your plans differed from His counsel?

DO AWAY WITH SELF-PROTECTION

Self-protecting strategies may have made life seem more livable (for the short haul), but they never bring true joy. Joy is only found in the abandonment of self-focused agendas and demands and the relinquishing of each one to Him. Those imaginary fiberglass walls we've built to insulate ourselves from disturbing truths are, in reality, the walls of a coffin, a place where faith, hope, and joy molder. Consider Paul's testimony:

- "But even if I am being poured out as a drink offering upon the sacrifice and service of your faith, I rejoice and share my joy with you all" (Philippians 2:17). Do you joyfully embrace the truth that your life is a sacrifice that is being poured out to serve others? How can your disappointments profit your husband or others and their faith?

- "I will most gladly spend and be expended for your souls" (2 Corinthians 12:15). What are you unwilling to relinquish for the sake of others? What will you spend to help your husband's soul prosper?

- "I am filled with comfort; I am overflowing with joy in all our affliction" (2 Corinthians 7:4). What is the source of your comfort? Would having your husband fulfill all your desires really bring you comfort and overflowing joy? What's the relationship between joy and affliction?

- "Now I rejoice in my sufferings for your sake, . . . filling up what is lacking in Christ's afflictions" (Colossians 1:24). Christ's afflictions were perfect—He finished everything God sent Him to do; and yet, there is a way in which your joyful suffering is used by God to draw others to Him. This happens, not when everything goes well and you're happy (What kind of testimony is that? Even unbelievers are happy when it's their party!), but when others see your struggles and get drenched in the overflow of your joyful response. Do you rejoice in your suffering? Do you see the redeeming power in it?

PURSUING A PASSIONATE LOVE

If you see the joy and redeeming power in suffering, you're now free to pursue both the Lord and your husband with a passionate love. Pursue your Lord because, when all this shadow finally becomes reality, He'll be the One to call you His own and seat you at the bridal table in His presence. All this muss and fuss is simply about getting you, His bride, ready for that day. Remember that even though preparing for a wedding can be troublesome, when the blessed day finally arrives, all the former hardships fade into insignificance.

- "'Let us rejoice and be glad and give the glory to Him, for the marriage of the Lamb has come and His bride has made herself ready.' It was given to her to clothe herself in fine linen, bright and clean; for the fine linen is the righteous acts of the saints" (Revelation 19:7–8). Is your heart captivated with the thought of that day? What righteous acts are you seeking to clothe yourself with? Although you've been clothed in the righteous acts of Jesus Christ, you can amplify this beauty, as your heart becomes increasingly more conformed to that of your Lord's.

- "As the bridegroom rejoices over the bride, so your God will rejoice over you" (Isaiah 62:5). Do you believe that God the Father rejoices over you as the bride for His Son? How does that truth enlighten and inspire you today?

- "I will betroth you to Me forever; yes, I will betroth you to Me in righteousness and in justice, in lovingkindness and in compassion, and I will betroth you to Me in faithfulness. Then you will know the Lord" (Hosea 2:19–20). Are you joyously anticipating the day when you will "know" the Lord? Are you thankful that He's betrothed you to Himself for eternal bliss? Do these truths captivate and motivate your heart?

You can pursue your husband now with unselfish love—love that gives and doesn't expect anything in return. You can woo him with a love that seeks to bless and gives the best to him, even when that means humbling yourself in service or speaking into a place of darkness in your lives. If your focus is on his ultimate holiness and joy in Christ, then it doesn't really matter if he fulfills all your preconceived expectations, does it? What really matters is whether you love him and you're fulfilling God's call in your life. Consider the following verses:

- "Love your enemies, and do good, and lend, expecting nothing in return; and your reward will be great, and you will be sons of the Most High; for He Himself is kind to ungrateful and evil men" (Luke 6:35). Even if your husband is your enemy, you're called to love him and do him good, without expecting anything in return. What would that kind of selfless love look like in your life?

- "Love your enemies, do good to those who hate you, bless those who curse you, pray for those who mistreat you. . . . Give to everyone who asks of you, and whoever takes away what is yours, do not demand it back" (Luke 6:27–28, 30). What do you demand? Do you function under a quid pro quo model? Do your actions say to your husband, "If you scratch my back, I'll scratch yours"? Or do you love him, do him good, bless him, and pray for him for Christ's sake, without demanding anything in return?

- "But God demonstrates His own love toward us, in that while we were yet sinners, Christ died for us. . . . For if while we were enemies we were reconciled to God through the death of His Son, much more, having been reconciled, we shall be saved by His life" (Romans 5:8, 10). God initiated and sustains a relationship with us through generous, condescending love. Are you impacted by this love that bowed down and pursued you? Will you do the same for your husband? Will you pursue areas where you've called a "truce" in order to either reconcile, grow in understanding, or willingly and joyfully sacrifice your desires to the Lord? Will you love your husband and the Lord this much?

- "For you know the grace of our Lord Jesus Christ, that though

He was rich, yet for your sake He became poor, so that you through His poverty might become rich" (2 Corinthians 8:9). Are you acquainted with the grace of the Lord? Is His gracious life flowing in you? Are you willing to become poor that your husband might become rich? What would embracing poverty of spirit look like in your marriage?

BE PREPARED, SELF-CONTROLLED, AND FULL OF HOPE

We've come a long way, haven't we? We've seen the preciousness of God's design for us as women who glorify Him and have been called to blessed roles. We've learned about the wonderful differences and similarities that exist between us and our husbands and how even these reflect or image our Creator. We've seen how sin blasted this image and how it is being restored in Christ. We've learned about our calling to oneness, love, and God-centered communication. So, what's left? Only for me to encourage you with the same words Peter used. He said:

> *Therefore, prepare your minds for action; be self-controlled; set your hope fully on the grace to be given you when Jesus Christ is revealed.* (1 Peter 1:13 NIV)

In the King James text of this verse, Peter instructed his readers to "gird up the loins" of their mind. This "girding up" referred to the practice of gathering up long flowing gowns so that quick, decisive movement wouldn't be hindered. It's easy to get entangled with the affairs of the world and the alluring desires we hear sung about the Vanity Fair of our hearts. *"You need a husband who . . .* (you fill in the blank) *or you can't be happy,"* they sing. Peter warns us that our minds are easily entrapped and ensnared. His point? Don't let your thoughts stray far from the truth, or you won't be able to respond proactively. If you're not careful, when it's time for you to jump, you'll be tripped up by the thoughts and desires you've given quarter to or you'll be sluggish and sleepy. It's the same sort of idea we find in Hebrews 12:1: "Let us also lay aside every encumbrance and the sin which so easily entangles us, and let us run with endurance the race that is set before us." In this case, we're warned against encumbrances and sins, while Peter warns us about thoughts or desires that entangle us.

- What thoughts entangle you? Do you think that you ought to be called something other than a companion or helper? Do you think that your husband was created for you, rather than you for him? Do you chafe against the thought of humble submission and view it as a slavish, patriarchal anachronism? Do you think you would be a better wife if you had a better husband?

PRACTICING SELF-CONTROL

Peter also taught his readers to be self-controlled. The most common default response when under pressure is to give in to self-indulgence. Self-indulgence can take many forms from hot fudge cakes to glasses of wine to romance novels or shopping sprees. There's nothing wrong with eating yummy desserts or shopping with friends, but if you're employing these diversions as an escape from difficulty, then they are your saviors and gods. When you find yourself in your most trying circumstance, that's the time to really buckle down and perhaps even avoid legitimate pleasures that might be all right for you when you're not really pressed.

Jesus faced strong temptation to please Himself when He was in the wilderness, hungry and alone. It was during that time of testing that He refused to turn stones into bread, even though at other times it was legitimate for Him to do so, as He multiplied bread for others. There's a certain temptation in seeking to satiate yourself when you're feeling put upon—it's this temptation that we must resist.

A SET HOPE

Finally, Peter tells us that we must set our "hope fully on the grace to be given . . . when Jesus Christ is revealed" (1 Peter 1:13 NIV). What is your hope set on? Is it set on your husband's performance? Is it even partially fixed on your own performance? Our only hope is grace! Our only source of comfort, strength, and joyful anticipation is the ongoing experience of God's favor and mercy. This grace is already yours now, in part, and will be completely, overwhelmingly yours, when you stand in His presence. Don't hope in your husband's reformation or even your own ability to change. Hope instead and only in the grace that has been brought to you through the perfections of Jesus Christ. This grace is yours now and will be unfailingly yours forever.

ARE WE THERE YET?

You and I are on a journey, traveling through an alien land on our way to Joy. Whether you have years and years to travel or just a few moments left, the anticipation of heaven's pleasures should captivate and inflame your heart. This anticipation should bubble out of your soul in incessant streams of gladness and impassioned service, in humble obedience and loving embracing of His call on your life. Whenever you need a landmark to encourage you along the way, look to the Garden of Gethsemane or gaze upon the Cross. What do you see? By faith, see your Savior, your heavenly Husband, hear His song, make it your own.

View Him prostrate in the garden, On the ground your Maker lies.
On the bloody tree behold Him, Sinner will this not suffice?
Lo! The incarnate God ascended, Pleads the merit of His blood.

Venture on Him, venture wholly.

Let no other trust intrude.

I will arise and go to Jesus, He will embrace me in His arms.

In the arms of my dear Savior,

O, there are ten thousand charms.[1]

When Wesley grasped my hand for comfort as we drove toward our day of fun, I learned a lesson. I discovered that travel is most enjoyable when shared with others. Yes, we're on a journey, but that journey will be especially hard if we try to go it alone. Take your husband's hand in yours, and help him hold the comforting, nail-scarred hand of your Savior. Grasp His hand, joy in His presence, patiently await your blissful reunion. "Are we there yet?" you may ask Him. "No," He'll reply, "not quite yet, my darling, but soon, soon."

Finding and Fulfilling Your Calling

1. *Psalm 45:13–15 reads, "The King's daughter is all glorious within; her clothing is interwoven with gold. She will be led to the King in embroidered work; the virgins, her companions who follow her, will be brought to You. They will be led forth with gladness and rejoicing; they will enter into the King's palace." What is your anticipation of entering the King's palace? Are you motivated with a hopeful joy and anticipation?*

2. *Summarize the teaching of this chapter in three or four sentences.*

3. *What does it mean to be called to help?*

207

4. *Go back over your summaries of all the preceding chapters and summarize what you've learned from this book. As you review your list, answer the following questions:*

   a. *What specific changes are you going to seek to make in faith?*

   b. *Being very specific, what will the first step look like?*

   c. *What problems do you anticipate?*

   d. *How will you overcome them?*

   e. *What is your goal?*

appendix A How You Can Know If You're a Christian

I'm so glad that you decided to turn to this page, way in the back of this book—and there are two reasons why I feel this way.

First of all, the truths that are contained in this book will be impossible for you to understand and follow if you aren't a Christian, and I want you to be able to know the joy of God-empowered change. But that really isn't the most important reason that I'm glad that you decided to turn here.

I'm also so pleased you turned to this page because I long for you to know the joy of peace with God and to have the assurance that your sins are forgiven. You see, if you've never really come to the place in your life where God opened your heart to the truth of His great love and sacrifice and your rebelliousness and need for forgiveness, you must question whether you really are a Christian.

Many people attend church or try to live "good" lives. We certainly aren't as bad as we could be . . . and so we think that like Patrick Swayze's character in *Ghost:* It doesn't really matter if we have trusted in Christ—if we're nice and we love people, God will accept us . . . right? You know, if it were up to me, if you had to live up to my standards, I might say that we're all OK. But, that's not the truth, and it isn't up to me. It's up to God . . . and His standards are different from mine. He says, "My ways are not your ways and My thoughts are not your thoughts."

The truth is that God is perfectly holy. That means He never thinks or does anything that is inconsistent with His perfection. He is pure and without fault of any kind. That's not because He gets up every morning and says, "I'll try to be good today." No, by His nature He is good and there's never a time when He isn't.

In addition to being perfectly holy, He is just. That means that He always sees that justice is served . . . or that those who deserve punishment will always receive it in the end. Now, I know that it may not seem that way to you, looking at things like we do from an earthly perspective, but let me assure you, the great Judge of all the earth will prevail. If God allowed people to get away with breaking His laws, then He wouldn't really be holy, would He?

In one sense, the truth of God's holiness and justice reassures us. The Hitlers of the world, even though they seemingly have escaped judgment here on earth, will stand before their Creator and will receive just what they deserve. But, in another sense, God's holiness and justice should make us all uncomfortable. That's because, even though we may not be as bad as we could be, we know that we all sin and that God hates sin. Very simply speaking, *sin is any violation of God's perfect standards.* His standards are contained in the Bible and were summed up in the Ten Commandments in the Old Testament.

Think for a moment about those commandments: Have you had any other gods in your life? Have you reverenced the Lord's Day and set it apart for Him? Have you always honored those in authority over you? Have you ever taken another's life or turned your back on someone who needed your protection? Have you ever desired someone who was not your spouse? Have you ever taken anything that wasn't yours to take? Have you ever told a lie or looked at something that someone else had and wanted it for yourself?

I'm sure, if you're like me, you'll say that you've probably broken each of God's commands at some time in your life. That means that there will come a time when you, too, will stand before God's judgment seat. But don't despair. If you know that you are a sinner, then there is hope for you because God is not only holy and just. He's also merciful.

God has mercy and pity on His people. He has immense love, and because of this, He made a way for you and me to come to Him. He did this without compromising His holiness and justice. You see, someone had to take the punishment for your sin. Someone had to die in your place. But who could do this and still maintain God's justice?

Every person who had ever lived had sinned and was therefore disqualified from taking someone else's punishment because they deserved punishment of their own. Only one Man could take this punishment. Only one Man was perfectly sinless and completely undeserving of punishment. That Man was Jesus Christ. Jesus Christ was both God (making Him perfectly sinless) and Man (making Him suitable as our stand-in). The Bible teaches that because of God's love for us, He sent His Son, Jesus Christ, to die in our place. On the cross, Jesus Christ took the punishment we deserved. Thus is God's justice served and His holiness upheld. That's why the Bible teaches that "while we were yet sinners, Christ died for us."

But that still leaves you with a problem. Perhaps as you are reading this you know that you are a sinner. You also believe that God is holy and just, and you are hoping that He is as merciful and loving as I've portrayed Him. What must you do? You must believe on Him. This means that you must believe in these truths and you must ask God to forgive you of all your sins. You can do this through prayer.

There aren't any special words that you must say. In fact, the Bible says that "all who call on the Name of the Lord will be saved." You can pray to Him, asking Him to forgive your sin because of Jesus' sacrifice. You can ask Him to make you His own. The Bible says, "If we confess our sins, He is faithful and just to forgive us our sins, and to cleanse us from all unrighteousness." You can rest in His truthfulness.

Now if you have become a Christian, you will want to live for Him in a way that pleases Him. In order to know how to do that, you must begin reading His Word. You should begin in the Gospel of John with the first chapter. As you read, pray that God will help you to understand. The next thing you should do is find a good, Bible-believing church and start attending it. A Bible-believing church is one that believes in the the doctrine of the Trinity (the Father, the Son, and the Holy Spirit are equally One God), believes that salvation is entirely a free gift of God, practices prayer and holiness, and preaches from God's Word (without any other books added).

If you've become a Christian through the ministry of this book, I would love to know so that I can rejoice with you. Please write to me through the publisher:

Moody Publishers
820 North LaSalle Boulevard
Chicago, Illinois 60610-3284

May God's richest blessings be yours as you bow humbly before His throne.

Your Wedding Invitation

To All the Hosts of Heaven,
Cherubim and Seraphim, Rulers and Authorities:
GOD MOST HIGH,
the Father of Glory and Ancient of Days
joyously announces the marriage of
His Only Begotten Son,
IMMANUEL,
The Lamb who was slain and lives again,
who bears the scars on His hands,
and _____,
who is joined with His Redeemed, Purified, and Perfect Bride.

On a day that has been determined in the counsel rooms of heaven when
she has fully clothed herself in His white linen and righteous acts.
The Spirit and the Bride say, "Come—Behold His wisdom! Behold His love!"

Let the one who is thirsty come and join in this celebration for all the ages,
drinking from the crystal clear River of Life and feasting at the table before
His throne.

Rejoice in Our joy and prepare yourself for this day,
You, Our blessed beloved, whom We have chosen and sealed for Ourselves.

Notes

Introduction: Something More than Tea and Cookies?

1. Cornish, Carol, *Women Helping Women,* ed. Elyse Fitzpatrick and Carol Cornish (Eugene, Ore.: Harvest House, 1997), 62.

Chapter 1: In His Image

1. Elizabeth Barrett Browning, *Aurora Leigh,* Book 7.

2. John Calvin, *Institutes of the Christian Religion,* ed. John T. McNeill, 2 vols., Library of Christian Classics (Philadelphia: Westminster, 1960), 1:188; italics added.

3. Wayne Grudem, *Bible Doctrine: Essential Teachings of the Christian Faith* (Grand Rapids: Zondervan, 1999), 116.

4. Ibid.

5. The expression "at last" is from John Piper, *Desiring God: Meditations of a Christian Hedonist* (Sisters, Ore.: Multnomah, 1996), 180.

6. Ibid., 50.

Chapter 2: His Companion, His Helper

1. Unpublished course notes, Dr. Iain Duguid, Associate Professor of Old Testament, Westminster Theological Seminary, Escondido, California.

2. Ibid.

3. Jay E. Adams, *A Theology of Christian Counseling: More than Redemption* (Grand Rapids: Zondervan, 1979), 126.

4. *Vine's Expository Dictionary of Biblical Words* (Nashville: Nelson, 1985), s.v. "comforter."

5. Ibid.

CHAPTER 3: A COVENANT OF COMPANIONSHIP

1. *Cast Away*, Twentieth Century Fox and Dreamworks, Los Angeles, California, 2000.

2. *Matthew Henry's Commentary on the Whole Bible*, New Modern Edition, electronic database (Peabody, Mass.: Hendrickson, 1991), comment on Ecclesiastes 4:9.

3. *The New Unger's Bible Dictionary* (Chicago: Moody, 1988), s.v. "covenant."

4. *Nelson's Illustrated Bible Dictionary* (Nashville: Nelson, 1986), s.v. "covenant."

5. Topical Sermons (Old Testament Texts); *Bands of Love: Hos. 11:4* from *Spurgeon's Sermons*, Electronic Database. Copyright (c) 1997 by Biblesoft.

6. J. Wilbur Chapman (1859–1918) and Rowland Hugh Prichard (1811–87), "Jesus! What a Friend for Sinners"; listed as "Our Great Savior" in *The Singing Church* (Carol Stream: Ill., Hope, 1985).

CHAPTER 4: "HERE, DEAR, HAVE A BITE"

1. *The Online Bible Thayer's Greek Lexicon and Brown Driver & Briggs Hebrew Lexicon*, (Ontario, Canada: Woodside Bible Fellowship, Ontario Bible Fellowship, 1993; licensed from the Institute for Creation Research) define this word in the following way: "to keep, to guard, to observe, to give heed, 1) to keep, to have charge of; 2) to keep, to guard, to keep watch and ward, to protect, to save life; watch, a watchman (participle); 3) to watch for, to wait for; 4) to watch, to observe; 5) to keep, to retain, to treasure up (in memory); 6) to keep (within bounds), to restrain; 7) to observe, to celebrate, to keep; (sabbath or covenant or commands), to perform (a vow); 8) to keep, to preserve, to protect; 9) to keep, to reserve."

2. Unpublished course notes, Dr. Iain M. Duguid, Associate Professor of Old Testament, Westminster Theological Seminar, Escodido, California. See also Gordon J. Wenham, *Word Biblical Commentary: Genesis 1–15* (Waco, Tex.: Word, 1987), note on Genesis 2:15, p. 67; and Bruce K. Waltke with Cathi J. Fredricks, *Genesis: A Commentary* (Grand Rapids: Zondervan, 2001), note on Genesis 2:15, p. 87. "The latter term [guard] entails guarding the garden against Satan's encroachment. . . As priest

and guardians of the garden, Adam and Eve should have driven out the serpent; instead it drives them out."

3. Iain Duguid, ibid.

4. Louis Berkhof, *Systematic Theology* (Grand Rapids: Eerdmans, 1932), 207.

5. *The Online Bible Thayer's Greek Lexicon and Brown Driver & Briggs Hebrew Lexicon.*

CHAPTER 5: WHAT GOD HAS JOINED TOGETHER

1. *The Online Bible Thayer's Greek Lexicon and Brown Driver & Briggs Hebrew Lexicon* Ontario, Canada: Woodside Bible Fellowship, Ontario Bible Fellowship, 1993; licensed from the Institute for Creation Research.

2. *Vine's Expository Dictionary of Biblical Words* (Nashville: Nelson, 1985).

3. Ibid.

4. *Jamieson, Fausset, and Brown Commentary,* Electronic Database. Copyright © 1997 by Biblesoft.

5. *The Online Bible Thayer's Greek Lexicon and Brown Driver & Briggs Hebrew Lexicon.*

CHAPTER 6: THE TWO SHALL BECOME ONE

1. Richard Baxter, *A Christian Directory* (Morgan, Pa.: Soli Deo Gloria, 1996), 432.

2. Charles Hodge, *Systematic Theology, Abridged Edition,* ed. Edward N. Gross (Phillipsburg, N.J.: Presb. & Ref., 1992), 168.

3. Wayne Mack, *Strengthening Your Marriage* (Phillipsburg, N.J.: Presb. & Ref., 1977), 97; (italics in original).

4. William Cutrer, M.D., and Sandra Glahn, *Sexual Intimacy in Marriage* (Grand Rapids: Kregel, 2001), 27.

5. Ibid., 53.

6. Gerhard von Rad, *Genesis: A Commentary* (Philadelphia: Westminster, 1976), 85; quoted in O. Palmer Robertson, *The Genesis of Sex: Sexual Relationships in the First Book of the Bible* (Phillipsburg, N.J.: Presb. & Ref., 2002), 4.

7. Cutrer and Glahn, *Sexual Intimacy in Marriage,* 35.

8. Ibid.; see also Ed Wheat, *Intended for Pleasure: Sex Technique and Sexual Fulfillment in Christian Marriage* (Grand Rapids: Revel, 1997).

9. For a fuller discussion of this subject, see Carol W. Cornish, "Why Women Should Counsel Women," in *Women Helping Women*, ed. Elyse Fitzpatrick and Carol Cornish (Eugene, Ore.: Harvest House, 1997).

CHAPTER 7: CALLED FOR HIS PURPOSE

1. "Happy Together" Written by Garry Bonner, Alan Gordon © 1966 Trio Music Company, Inc., Alley Music Corp. Copyright renewed. All rights reserved. Used by Permission.

2. "K" in Rev. John Rippon, *A Selection of Hymns from the Best Authors*, 1787. The text used in this chapter is taken from *Worship and Service Hymnal* (Chicago: Hope, 1968).

3. *Vine's Expository Dictionary of Biblical Words* (Nashville: Nelson, 1985).

4. *Vincent's Word Studies of the New Testament*, Electronic Database, copyright © 1997 by Biblesoft.

5. *Barnes' Notes*, Electronic Database. Copyright © 1997 by Biblesoft.

6. *Merriam-Webster's Dictionary of Synonyms* (Springfield, Mass.: Merriam-Webster, 1984).

7. John Piper, *Desiring God: Meditations of a Christian Hedonist* (Sisters, Ore.: Multnomah, 1986), 45.

CHAPTER 8: BECAUSE HE FIRST LOVED US

1. Charles Hodge, *Systematic Theology, Abridged Edition*, ed. Edward N. Gross, (Phillipsburg, N. J.: Presb. & Ref., 1992), 340.

2. For a more thorough treatment of the role that idolatry plays in our hearts, see my *Idols of the Heart: Learning to Long for God Alone* (Phillipsburg, N.J.: Presb. & Ref., 2001).

3. Matthew Bridges, Godfrey Thring, and George Elvey, *Crown Him with Many Crowns*, 1868.

4. *Vine's Expository Dictionary of Biblical Words* (Nashville: Nelson, 1985).

5. "Christ's New Commandment: John 13:34, 35," *Spurgeon's Encyclopedia of Sermons* (italics added), *PC Study Bible, Spurgeon's Sermons*, Electronic Database, copyright © 1997 by Biblesoft.

CHAPTER 9: LEARNING THE STEPS OF THE DANCE

1. See my *Idols of the Heart: Learning to Long for God Alone* (Phillipsburg, N.J.: Presb. & Ref., 2001).

2. *The Online Bible Thayer's Greek Lexicon and Brown Driver & Briggs Hebrew Lexicon,* Ontario, Canada: Woodside Bible Fellowship, Ontario Bible Fellowship, 1993; licensed from the Institute for Creation Research.

3. Unpublished course notes, Dr. Iain M. Duguid, Associate Professor of Old Testament at Westminster Theological Seminary, Escodido, California.

4. *The Online Bible Thayer's Greek Lexicon and Brown Driver & Briggs Hebrew Lexicon.*

5. Rebecca Jones, "Submission," an Internet article published in the CBMW magazine and on the web site www.spirit-wars.com. Rebecca Jones is a thoughtful and erudite Christian woman whose insights, particularly on this topic, I value.

6. John Piper and Wayne Grudem, ed., *Recovering Biblical Manhood and Womanhood: A Response to Evangelical Feminism* (Wheaton, Ill.: Crossway, 1993), 196.

7. Ibid., 197

CHAPTER 10: CREATED TO COMMUNICATE

1. Lise Eliot, *What's Going On in There? How the Brain and Mind Develop in the First Five Years of Life* (New York: Bantam, 1999), pp. 364f.

2. Ibid., 379.

3. Ibid.

4. Sally P. Springer and Georg Deutsch, *Left Brain, Right Brain,* rev. ed. (New York: W. H. Freeman, 1985), 185.

5. Ibid., 381.

6. Roberta Michnick Golinkoff and Kathy Hirsh-Pasek, *How Babies Talk: The Magic and Mystery of Language in the First Three Years of Life* (New York: Dutton, 1999), 139.

7. Werner Neuer, *Man and Women in Christian Perspective* (Wheaton, Ill.: Crossway, 1991), 42. This book is a fascinating study of the differences between men and women both scientifically and biblically. See also Eliot, *What's Going On in There?* 430; Springer and Deutsch, *Left Brain, Right Brain,* 184; Golinkoff and Hirsh-Pasek, *How Babies Talk,* 139; and Clare Shaw, *Talking and Your Child* (London: Headway, Hodder & Stoughton, 1993), 115.

8. Iain M. Duguid, *Living in the Gap Between Promise and Reality: The Gospel According to Abraham* (Phillipsburg, N.J.: Presb. & Ref., 1999), 64.

9. Wayne Grudem, *Bible Doctrine: Essential Teaching of the Christian Faith* (Grand Rapids: Zondervan, 1999), 258.

10. One of the best books I've found about the proper method of confessing sin and confronting offenses in others is Ken Sande, *Peacemaker: A Biblical Guide to Resolving Personal Conflict* (Grand Rapids: Baker, 1997).

11. Jay Adams, *Christian Counselor's Commentary: Proverbs* (Woodruff, S.C.: Timeless Texts, 1997), 132; emphasis in original.

12. One of the best books on this topic that I've found is Paul David Tripp, *War of Words: Getting to the Heart of Your Communication Struggles* (Phillipsburg, N.J.: Presb. & Ref., 2000).

CHAPTER 11: HELPING YOUR HUSBAND BELIEVE

1. From private correspondence with Dennis E. Johnson, Ph.D., Professor of Practical Theology, Westminster Theological Seminary, Escondido, California. Other commentators write: "The author's point is not to forbid verbal testimony by Christian wives but to suggest tactfully that such testimony is not obligatory, and sometimes not helpful" (J. Ramsey Michaels, *1 Peter*, Word Biblical Commentary, vol. 49 [Waco: Word, 1988]), 158. "The word (ho logos) of Gospel message claims men's obedience . . . but the presentation of it in the discourse (logos) by missionary or teacher is not the only means by which men may be won to . . . it" (E. G Selwyn, *The First Epistle of Saint Peter: The Greek Text with Introduction, Notes, and Essays*, 2d ed. [London: Macmillan, 1947], 183).

CHAPTER 12: WOMEN WHO HOPE IN GOD

1. "Come Ye Sinners, Poor and Needy," words by Joseph Hart (1712–68), public domain. Thanks to Fernando Ortega for introducing an updated version of this song on his album, Storm, © 2002 Word Entertainment.

MOODY
PUBLISHERS
THE NAME YOU CAN TRUST®

HELPER BY DESIGN TEAM

ACQUIRING EDITOR:
Elsa Mazon

COPY EDITOR:
Anne Scherich

BACK COVER COPY:
Julie-Allyson-Ieron, Joy Media

COVER DESIGN:
Ragont Design

INTERIOR DESIGN:
Ragont Design

PRINTING AND BINDING:
Color House Graphics, Inc.

The typeface for the text of this book is
Berkeley